Lesley Ellen Harris enlightens every virtual stakeholder in the "cyberspace goldrush" from cultural repositories, such as museums and libraries, to the unpublished poet, about their rights, responsibilities and potential gain in this "new territory." We need this book!

Katherine Jones-Garmil, Assistant Director
Peabody Museum of Archaeology and Ethnology
Harvard University

New rules, new media. As the digital universe unfurls, we need to understand how the rules that are forming affect us. This book helps do just that.

Ted Leonsis, President and CEO
AOL Studios

This very readable book reminds us that we are all both potential creators and users of digital property. Essential reading for everyone connected to the information highway. And, you don't have to go to law school to understand its message!

Karen Adams, Executive Director
Canadian Library Association

Lesley Harris' book shows why protecting intellectual property in cyberspace has become the publishing industry's top priority. Without safeguards for digital property, the Internet cannot realize its enormous potential as a commercial, educational and entertainment medium.

Pat Schroeder, President and CEO
Association of American Publishers

This book is the first to explain the nature, value and marketing of intellectual property in the new digital age. There are lots of legal treatises on the subject, but *Digital Property* is the only work that is both accurate and readable for a broad international audience.

Ken Wasch, President
Software Publishers Association
(Washington, D.C.)

Digital Property

CURRENCY OF THE 21ST CENTURY

LESLEY ELLEN HARRIS

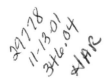

 **McGraw-Hill Ryerson**

TORONTO NEW YORK BURR RIDGE BANGKOK BOGOTÁ
CARACAS LISBON LONDON MADRID MEXICO CITY MILAN
NEW DELHI SEOUL SINGAPORE SYDNEY TAIPEI

McGraw-Hill Ryerson Limited

A Subsidiary of The McGraw-Hill Companies

300 Water Street, Whitby, Ontario L1N 9B6
http://www.mcgrawhill.ca

Digital Property: Currency of the 21st Century

The material in this publication is provided for information purposes only. Laws, regulations, and procedures are constantly changing, and the examples given are intended to be general guidelines only. This book is sold with the understanding that neither the author nor the publisher is engaged in rendering professional advice. It is recommended that legal, accounting, tax, and other advice or assistance be obtained before acting on any information contained in this book. Personal services of a competent professional should be sought.

The author, publisher, and all others directly or indirectly involved with this publication do not assume any responsibility or liability, direct or indirect, to any party for any loss or damage by errors or omissions, regardless of the cause, as a consequence of using this publication, nor accept any contractual, tortious, or other form of liability for the publication's contents or any consequences arising from its use.

ISBN: 0-07-552846-0

2 3 4 5 6 7 8 9 0   W   6 5 4 3 2 1 0 9

Printed and bound in Canada

Care has been taken to trace ownership of copyright material contained in this text; however, the publisher welcomes any information that enables them to rectify any reference or credit for subsequent editions.

Canadian Cataloguing in Publication Data

Harris, Lesley Ellen
  Digital property : currency of the 21st century

Includes index.
ISBN 0-07-552846-0

1. Copyright and electronic data processing.   2. Intellectual property.   I. Title.

KI401.H37 1997   346.04'8   C97-932362-2

Publisher: **Joan Homewood**
Editor: **Erin Moore**
Production Coordinator: **Jennifer Burnell**
Editorial Services: **Scott Mitchell**
Cover Design: **Jack Steiner**
Back Cover Photograph: **Frank Tancredi**
Interior Design: **Dianna Little**
Composition: **Bookman Typesetting Co.**
Printer: **Webcom**
Typefaces: **Meridien**

Contents

Preface

Digital property. It's a concept, a creation, an asset — and definitely an expression you should add to your vocabulary, right away. That's because you're about to hear a lot about digital property. And not merely in this book.

My guess is you've already heard about the digital economy and digital media and digital everything else. You might even have come across the term *digital property*, or perhaps *digital real estate*, and that may be why you picked up this book. Whether you already understand the ones and zeros that constitute something digital, or you're looking for some clarity about the unlimited onramps to the world of the Internet, or you've heard there's money to be made from digital property, this book will introduce you to a new world. This is an invisible world, a fascinating invisible world about information and content and education and culture and entertainment and business. It is a world about the importance of intangible property, and it is the world in which we now live and will continue to rapidly prosper in.

This book was originally titled "Intellectual Property: Currency of the Twenty-First Century." My guess is that you would not have picked up a book with that title. Personally, I'm not convinced that I could have written an interesting book with that title. But no matter what it's called, that's what this book is about. Digital property is what I refer to as "the coming of age" of intellectual property. The concept of intellectual property goes back many centuries, but it wasn't until the evolution of digital media, and more recently the popularization of computer networks like the Internet, that it began to have an enormous impact in the workplace and at home and everywhere else. And now, intellectual property, which was once primarily the concern of inventors, artists, Hollywood studios, and the sophisticated businessperson, is everyone's concern. That's why this book was written, and, I assume, why it is being read.

I wrote this book because I find the new media exciting and also because, after the last real estate boom, I got tired of hearing people say how they should have bought real estate when prices were low in order to have profited during the ensuing boom. In terms of new media, I believe that prices are low, sometimes nonexistent (that is, the content of the new media is accessible by the public for free), but we are on an upward trend. Now is the time to comprehend the economy of the twenty-first century and be prepared for it. In brief, buy now, sell later. Understand the currency of the next century and you'll be positioned to gain from it.

This is a general interest book. In a bookstore, it could be shelved equally as well with business books, or computer/Internet books, or legal books, or reference books, or in the arts and entertainment section. It is a book I hope you will pick up on a Sunday afternoon, maybe at the beach, or at your summer or winter home. It was written on many Sunday afternoons (and mornings and evenings, not to mention the other six days of the week!) with the broadest audience in mind — from small business people, to corporate CEOs, to investors and entrepreneurs looking for new business opportunities and following the lead of savvy investors who, since the late 1980s, have been quietly acquiring electronic rights and purchasing intellectual property. It was written for creators and artists in all disciplines, as well as for consumers, publishers, and distributors of cultural, entertainment, business and educational products. It was written for students, educators, librarians, archivists, and museum workers. This book is for everyone. And it is written for today's as well as tomorrow's world.

Notwithstanding the rapid expansion of the digital economy and digital media, the need for a book on digital property was not immediate. It took over two years to find the exact publishing deal I was interested in signing. Initially, I was told by one book publisher that unlike most books, this one would have to be sold twice (with author royalties only attaching one time!). First, I would have to sell the fact that intellectual property is an essential issue to know about in the twenty-first century. Second, I would have to sell my book as the source of that information. I think, however, the topic has over the past few years sold itself (and steadfastly continues to do so). Now it is up to me, and my current publisher, to sell this book as the source of the information you seek.

I have tried to make this book as current as possible. However, the information in it reflects the technology, law, culture, and society as it exists at the time of writing. In terms of technology, law, and practical effects on global culture and on society as a whole, it is an understatement to say that this is a rapidly changing field. This book aims to provide a foundation for this topic. It is an evolving book, much like new media itself, and should be read as such.

Many Web site addresses or URLs (pronounced by some people as "earls") are set out in this book. It is likely that some URLs will no longer be valid when you look them up. Where this happens, use one of the Internet search engines to locate similar Web sites. It is also possible that relevant sites were overlooked, or appeared after the book was published. Feel free to email me about any new or additional Web sites.

Throughout this book, I questioned my ability to write it. Although I am a creator as well as a copyright and new media lawyer, I have no special background in economics or business, and yet many of the principles and thoughts set out in the following pages relate to the new information economy, to changing business models and industry standards. Nor do I have special knowledge in the area of communications, and yet much of what I say relates to the revamping of communications policy, the way the world is structured, and the way we share information and knowledge. By declaring this, I feel more comfortable in setting out my perspectives, and I hope that my rather simplified view of things will in fact help others understand the new world in which we now live.

I find the Internet and other new media fascinating. I am constantly absorbed by articles in print and electronic publications that concern new media, and I often interrupt and join in on conversations in restaurants and at social gatherings when I hear people talking about the Internet. I publish on the Internet through my own Web site (*http://copyrightlaws.com/*) and the Web sites of others, and I "consume" a variety of content on the Internet, for personal and business purposes. As a creator, owner, and user of content, I personally have much to gain from the new media, as will many readers of this book.

In addition, as a copyright and new media lawyer, I represent clients who create and consume intellectual property, including book, magazine, music, and online publishers, writers, photographers, filmmakers, designers, consultants and Internet-related businesspeople, and others who work in telecommunications, cartography, government, education, information studies, archival institutions, museums, various trade associations and organizations, and creators' unions. As such, I have been exposed to a large variety of legal and business issues relating to intellectual property and new media, and I share my experiences in this book. In my work for these clients, I am continually faced with the need for "creative" problem solving and for anticipating the future, in drafting, negotiating, and reviewing agreements, examining digital copyright issues on an international level, and suggesting how the copyright laws should be amended to protect my clients' interests in new media.

I am also exposed to various electronic rights concerns of creators and consumers of intellectual property through the frequently asked questions (FAQ) section of the Web site for my other book, *Canadian Copyright Law* (*http://www.mcgrawhill.ca/copyrightlaw/*) as well as through the questions I receive from readers of articles I write for various publications on this subject. I frequently speak on this topic, and I have been impressed by the increased level of knowledge in audiences over the past several years. Many of the questions I'm asked are answered in this book. Lastly, I continue to be intrigued by the schemes I talk about in the "get paid" portions of this book which deal with ways for making money from the Internet and other new media. In fact, I'm intrigued enough to try some of them myself, such as selling content from a Web site and electronic publishing. I hope that this book will encourage you in the same manner.

Lesley Ellen Harris
lesley@copyrightlaws.com

Acknowledgments

Thank you to all the people who supported me along the way, whether it was to free my time to write, pat me on the back, listen to my ideas, discuss my questions, or review parts of this book. As no book is written alone, this one was written with the help of numerous people, many of whom I know only through the touch of my keyboard in cyberspace, and many who responded to my email at all hours of the day and night in all parts of the world to talk about new media and technology and intellectual property. I would also like to express appreciation to my clients in my legal practice who have exposed me to a variety of interesting issues and continually make me think about the notion of digital property.

Specifically, I would like to thank Ken Wasch, Lisa Balaban, Gay Young, Garry Neil, as well as those who provided me with valuable research, including Colin Ground, Greg Segal, Evan Shapiro, Lesley Lizmore, Javier Castro-Aliaga, Alex Dey, and Jennifer Howe, and those who answered specific questions like John P. Mason and David Ellis. And, of course, my sincere thanks to Julia Woods, Joan Homewood, Sharon Hudson, Sharon Budnick, Suzanne Tobin, and others at McGraw-Hill Ryerson, and to my editor, Scott Mitchell.

The *WIPO Copyright Treaty* and *WIPO Performances and Phonograms Treaty* are reprinted by permission of the International Bureau of the World Intellectual Property Organization.

P A R T I

The Content of the Information Revolution

Hot Property

I can't understand it. I can't even understand the people who can understand it.

— Queen Juliana of the Netherlands

Like everyone else, at times I can be accused of living in my own world. As a creative or fiction writer, this seems to be accepted. My friends and colleagues who know me as a writer understand that my best friend can be a character I've created for purposes of a novel or screenplay. And they understand and admire how I can create an *imaginary* world that exists only within the pages. People even ask me at dinner parties (sometimes to my annoyance) to describe this *imaginary* world which I often share only with my word processor. There is some intrigue, some mystique to it. People value what's in my mind and want to be a part of it.

As a copyright lawyer, I can also be accused of living in my own world, but a different world. My friends and acquaintances who know me as a lawyer do not understand why I can't help them with the purchase of their new house, their will or divorce. They don't understand why at dinner parties I'm always talking about the Internet, email, digital this and digital that. At social gatherings, my friends introduce me as an intellectual property lawyer, and in response I get hmms and haws. Then the person I've just met will tell me about this great idea they have and ask how I can help them make a fortune from it. And when it's my turn to talk, I go off on this tangent about the notion of intellectual property, *intangible* property, and how valuable it's becoming. I can sense that the listener is intrigued, and perhaps a little mystified. I also see nods, and a yearning to understand more, more about my world, this world of *intangible* property.

So, I live in two worlds, the imaginary and the intangible, two worlds yearning for left- and right-brain attention. And two worlds that are colliding in the digital world.

My Digital World

In my digital world, you will be introduced to many new concepts. At times you will have to be patient as the concepts interconnect, and the one being explained may not make much sense until the next one is described, but I promise to start at square one in the hope that you can follow my story. In many ways, this book is not unlike a story, a work of fiction, or perhaps science fiction, because it deals with the real and the unreal, the proven and the unproven. It started as an idea (which you'll soon know is difficult to protect under the law), turned into a book proposal, then a manuscript, and now a print book. Of course, there is also a Web site or *digital* site for it (*http://www.mcgrawhill.ca/digitalproperty*).

In my world, intellectual property is hot property. Society as we now know it is undergoing a radical change, and intellectual property, hiply referred to as IP (pronounced "aye pee"— but not to be confused with the acronym for Internet Protocol), is an integral part of this change. Society now recognizes that information is quickly becoming the basis for the new economy, and IP is the new economy's strongest currency.

But What Is IP?

Many times when I have uttered the phrase "intellectual property" over the past dozen or more years, I've been treated like I'm speaking another language, I'm from another planet, I'm some sort of intellectual snob, or I sell real estate to very well-heeled clients. Once in a while there is a nod from someone who creates intellectual property, who sells or buys it, makes money from it, or perhaps pirates it! One thing I can tell you is that there is nothing inherently *intellectual* about intellectual property. IP is a finger painting created by a child or a letter written to your aunt. It is the article you write for your synagogue, church, or office newsletter. It is an email message, or the text or image you post on your Web site. It is also the basis of the new economy, and of course, of the high-paced entertainment and computer software industries. Even those who can only dream of owning a house in the next century may own this other sort of property.

Until recently, intellectual property existed primarily in the form of books, newspapers, magazines, sound recordings, paintings, and films. Creators of these works were concerned with being able to control them and collect payment for their use. For instance, when a book is photocopied or a film is shown in a theater, its rights holder has the right to permit that use and to be paid for it. Of course, many unauthorized uses also take place. Although the media are changing from print and analog-based to digital, many of the same concerns remain. Owners of new forms of IP, including computer software and CD-ROMs, as well as text, images, animation, audio, and film clips on the Internet, want to control and to be paid for the use of their works. However, as with the traditional (print and analog) media, it is difficult to monitor unauthorized uses. The "stealing" of intellectual property has become even easier with digital technology — electronically copying someone else's work takes very little time and almost no effort, often costs nothing or very little, and the reproductions are as perfect as the originals.

Digital Property

Because so much intellectual property or "content" now exists in a digital form and is part of our everyday lives, I often refer to intellectual property as *digital property*, a term that seems more accessible. Of course, digital property is only one piece of the puzzle when examining IP, but for most purposes of this book, it is one of the most relevant pieces.

Digital property is the content on your computer or on the Internet. But digital property, as you will see in later chapters, does not have to exist in a digital form. A photograph or a list of your friends or customers can also be digital property, as it can be converted into a digital form. There are lots of other examples throughout this book. In short, all IP that can be digitized or exists in a digital form or is generated by a digital means (e.g., through computer software) is digital property.

A New Language

As you might already have guessed, this book is about speaking a new language. Fortunately, even those with lousy aptitudes for new languages need not shy away. This new language uses the alphabet we're already using and uses many of the same words. What's new about this language is that it applies to a new technology and to a new economy. What's cool about it is that you'll learn a new lingo while speaking English.

And if you're one of those people who have always had trouble learning new languages, take some comfort in the fact that this is one you already speak. Have you ever uttered the word *Internet*? That is part of the new language I'm speaking about. And in case you didn't know this tidbit of information, the word *Internet* was not even mentioned in the mass media until the end of 1993. Now are you more encouraged that you'll have a chance with this "new" language?

Is There a Name for Now?

> *I don't need any new ideas. I'm confused enough already.*
>
> — Patrick McMullen, in *Brothers McMullen* (written by Edward J. Burns)

Many different terms are being used when people speak about this new era, such as *digital economy* and *information highway*. Although these two terms may not encompass exactly the same ingredients, they overlap because they both involve *new media* (sorry, another new concept!). But let's go back a step and understand these new terms.

One of the earlier and most media-hyped terms we've been confronted with is the *information highway* (also called the *information superhighway*, the *infobahn*, or simply the *I-way*). There is no definitive definition of the information highway. However, we can speak of the I-way as both a place where we store and find content (like books, music, photographs, films) and as a route by which content is distributed. The term *digital economy* has to do with the fact that we will make money from the I-way. Both of these terms are fundamental to the discussions in this book.

The I-way encompasses a vast variety of works and modes of disseminating and accessing (in the broadest terms) these works. Although we consider the I-way as "new," a recent U.S. task force report on *Intellectual Property and the National Information Infrastructure* reminds us that much of its structure, including the Internet, has been in place for some time:

> **An information infrastructure already exists, but it is not integrated into a whole. Telephones, televisions, radios, computers and fax machines are used every day to receive, store, process, perform, display and transmit data, text, voice, sound and images in homes and businesses throughout the country. Fiber optics, wires, cables, switches, routers, microwave networks, satellites and other communications technologies currently connect telephones, computers and fax machines. The NII [national information infrastructure] of tomorrow, however, will be much more than these separate communications networks; it will integrate them into an advanced high-speed, interactive, broad-**

band, digital communications system. Computers,
telephones, televisions, radios, fax machines and
more will be linked by the NII, and users will
be able to communicate and interact with other
computers, telephones, televisions, radios, fax
machines and more — all in digital format.[1]

In practical terms, the I-way allows you to "electronically" communicate with your colleagues, friends, and employers, send letters and photographs, get news, jointly create stories, work documents, music and drawings, find answers to questions, solve problems, gamble, shop, be entertained, publish books and magazines, perform concerts with instrumentalists in different cities, plan budgets, advertise, and get educated. These activities could be accomplished through email, the Web, other parts of the Internet, and online services like America Online and the Microsoft Network.

The Internet

In many situations, including in this book, references to the I-way are in fact focused upon the Internet ("the Net"), the global network of networks that connects computers around the world. For purposes of this book, the terms *I-way* and *Internet* are often used interchangeably, although the I-way may in fact encompass more than the Net.

The most well-known part of the Internet has become the World Wide Web ("the Web"). In fact, many people use the terms *Internet* and *Web* interchangeably (as I do in this book). The beauty of the Web and the reason why it has become the most popular and "populated" part of the Internet is that its content is readily accessible, usually graphically displayed, and can easily be navigated by the click of your computer mouse. The Web has been called the world's largest library because it contains such a wealth of text, images, music, video clips, recorded interviews, speeches, and conversations, which is often available for free to the public. The Web has also become the most popular Internet arena for buying and selling content. Other components of the Net include the infinite number of newsgroups, BBSes (bulletin board systems), and online chat groups.

A Web site is a collection of "pages" on the Web, and these pages contain content (text, images, animation, music, audio and video clips, and so on). The address for a Web site is called a Uniform Resource Locator (URL). A Web site may be viewed by using a computer software program called a *browser*, and viewing Web sites is often referred to as browsing, surfing, or accessing the Web.

An *intranet* is a "closed" or "internal" computer network within an organization, which may only be accessible to certain persons, like the employees of the organization. An *extranet* is similar to an intranet; however, it is usually accessible to certain suppliers and customers/clients of an organization, as well as to employees.

Content and Digital Property

> *To err is human but to really foul things up requires a computer.*
> — Anonymous

The Internet contains cultural, educational, commercial, and information products often referred to as "content." Content is a magazine article or a photograph, an audio or video clip, as well as a Web site, multimedia conference presentation, CD-ROM, or computer software. Content is IP and digital property. Content is the "information" on the Internet, the *packaged* information which is available to us.

What Is New Media?

New media is a term often used in the digital economy. I believe that new media is any media that didn't exist in the eyes of the general public more than five years ago — as well as tomorrow's media — so we're talking about CD-ROMs, DVDs (digital versatile discs, originally called digital video discs), Web sites, and e-zines (electronic magazines), as well as photographs, animation, text, computer games, films, and audio recordings accessed through the Internet. All this "stuff" that is fascinating, confusing, and bombarding our lives is new media.

What Is Digital Technology?

The Internet is based on digital technology. Digital technology means the storage, reproduction, and transmission of *any* piece of information — data, sound, video, text, graphics — in the form of digits, in binary code consisting of zeros and ones. The digital pattern can be transmitted by satellite, optical fiber, coaxial cable, microwave link, and conventional phone lines, and can then be converted back to its original format. Digital information is usually only machine-readable, and must be converted by the machine into some other form before it can be understood by human beings.

The terms *digital* and *electronic* are used interchangeably in this book.

What Is Electronic Commerce?

Electronic commerce is about making money on the Internet. Electronic commerce is any sort of transaction by which a product or service is purchased and paid for through the Internet. For instance, if you buy a book from the Amazon.com online bookstore, or you purchase a T-shirt from an online clothing store, then that is a transaction involving electronic commerce. The most common online purchases are for computer software, music recordings, and travel services, as well as books and magazines. Buying and selling through the Internet using electronic commerce is a natural market for IP, since the product itself (the digitized text, photograph, audio or film clip) can often be distributed or delivered through the Internet. *Digital commerce*, as a subset of electronic commerce, is a term used to describe IP that is purchased *and* delivered online.

Currently, the most common method of payment in online transactions is by credit card (the relevant information, such as card number, cardholder name, and expiry date, is keyed into a "secure" area in a Web site which uses special computer software so that others cannot have access to that information). Alternative methods of payment are gaining popularity, including several forms of electronic money or cybercash, whereby one purchases a certain amount of cybercash in advance which can then be used to buy goods and services on the Internet. Electronic commerce is still in its infancy but seems to have support from many of the major banks and credit card companies who are participating in its development. Although its future is uncertain, certain aspects of electronic commerce — shopping for books, magazines, music, and computer software, for instance — seem to be gaining popularity with the enthusiastic shopping public.

Intangible Property

The most difficult concept to be presented in this book is the concept of invisible or intangible property. This concept relates to the notion of IP (particularly copyright) being about "property rights" given to information, but not existing in information itself. Whereas *information* itself — ideas, news, history, facts — is in the public domain and free to be used by anyone in any manner, property rights in the *expression* of information are protected by the law, specifically under copyright law. To illustrate, copyright law does not protect the actual idea of building a deck for your house. However, it does protect the words you use in a book describing your idea, or the particular expression of that information. I will elaborate on this concept in chapter 6, "The Legal Protection of Digital Property."

Understanding the Notion of IP

I don't get ulcers, I give them.
— David Sarnoff

Let's go back for a moment and examine the notion of IP and technology. Even before the digital explosion, IP increasingly found its value in new technologies, and this has been true of technological advances throughout this century. We have seen a number of people rise to the top of their technology (so to speak) because they understood the notion of IP. Look at David Sarnoff who introduced television sets into our homes, or Bill Gates, who popularized Microsoft Windows, the user interface used by ninety percent of the world's computers. These are examples of two people who understood the value of software as opposed to hardware, the content for their products, the packaging of information — this is the property that made Gates and Sarnoff hot (not to mention wealthy). They understood that software (content) is more important than hardware.

This book attempts to give you the same understanding that made Sarnoff, Gates, and others successful in their relative industries — the understanding that IP (especially in digital form) has great value. Just as wealth is built in a traditional economy not merely by understanding the value of a dollar but by what one does with the dollar, so in the digital economy to create wealth you must first understand the currency of that economy — intellectual property — and what to do with it. With that understanding, you will be able to participate in, and profit from, the new economy.

Understanding the Root Value of IP

Intangible property such as IP derives its value in a different manner from *tangible* property (like houses and jewelry). For example, IP is usually consumed by more than one person at the same time. Computer software, a Web site, or a video can be used simultaneously by many people, unlike a piece of jewelry. Further, the very value of IP may come from its ability to be multiplied in identical copies and simultaneously used by many consumers in the same format or in different formats (e.g., in a print book form, as an audiotape, or as a television series based on the book). Thus, a single book or video or photograph does not by itself necessarily form the basis for the value of the IP; what must be evaluated is the capacity to duplicate the work for use by many consumers simultaneously in many different forms and media, as well as the capacity to duplicate and resell the rights in the work. These concepts will be revisited throughout this book.

A Final Word

As you can see, getting on with this story is not an easy job. The technology itself is confusing enough. If you've ever tried to buy a computer, you know exactly what I mean — the gigs and megs and RAM. And now you are being told that invisible property is the valuable property of the future. But that is precisely why this book was written: to demystify some of the essential concepts, to identify the resources, to unveil the wealth of the new millennium, to provide some answers, to create order, to help you develop your own feel for digital property, and to suggest elements of a strategy to make a few bucks from your digital property, the property that is the currency of the twenty-first century, the hot property.

I can only undertake this somewhat daunting task because I truly believe that intellectual property is important and fascinating (I know . . . I live in my own world). I am also aware that IP will not improve your sex life. It won't help you live longer, enrich your personal relationships, find answers to the meaning of life, save money on your taxes, make you shine in your kid's eyes, or make you rich in twenty-one days or less. On the other hand, perhaps it could do some or all of those things. Now I can and will make one promise. I promise you, that like death and taxes, you will not be able to avoid IP in the twenty-first century. So welcome to my world. And welcome to the twenty-first century.

End Notes

1. *Intellectual Property and the National Information Infrastructure*, Report of the Working Group on Intellectual Property Rights, Bruce A. Lehman, Assistant Secretary of Commerce and Commissioner of Patents and Trademarks, Chair, Information Infrastructure Task Force, Ronald H. Brown, Secretary of Commerce Chair, July 1994, *http://www.uspto.gov/web/offices/com/doc/ipnii/*.

CHAPTER 2

Picasso Created IP, but Do You?

The trouble, Mr. Goldwyn, is that you are only interested in art and I am only interested in money.

— George Bernard Shaw (to Sam Goldwyn, Hollywood producer)

Content, IP, digital property — we've now had a glimpse of these concepts and terms, but what does this all really mean? This chapter gives "live" examples of valuable digital property and looks at what individuals, organizations, institutions, and governments are digitizing. Subsequent chapters will explore your own digital opportunities.

Digital Assets

Your digital property can be valuable to you or your company. One way of describing this valuable property is with the term *digital asset*. A digital asset is anything of value that (1) exists in digital form, (2) is generated by digital means, or (3) may have value if adapted to digital form.

(1)   Assets Existing in Digital Form

The contents of your Web site or electronic newsletter exist in a digital form, as do the photographs you've scanned into your computer. Documents or conference presentations stored in your computer are in a digital form.

(2)   Assets Generated by Digital Means

You may already have a digital asset consisting of a list of contact information for friends or clients, created and stored in a database in your computer. This list may indicate which friends or clients requested to be notified about a certain event such as the publication of a new book, the release of a new product by your company, or updates to your Web site. By pressing a few buttons, you may be able to "generate" this customized list of people, thereby creating a new digital asset. Further, a new digital asset can be created by a statistical calculation prepared with the aid of computer software, or a translation of a document (from French to English, for example) prepared by computer translation software.

(3)   Assets Adapted to Digital Form

You do not need an Internet presence to have digital assets. Any works such as reports, articles, photographs, and comic strips which exist in a print form and which you can digitize by scanning or keying into your computer are digital assets, as they are capable of being adapted to a digital form and may have value in digital form. Even a list of contacts from your Rolodex that can be typed into your contact management software or database program is a digital asset.

Your Natural IP Resources

A lot of works that you don't think about may have value in digital form, and this and subsequent chapters will help you realize the potential value of your digital assets. What's important to know is that you have a quantity of "natural resources" that are, or can be turned into, important digital assets. They may be hidden or visible, and they may also have more value than you realize, both for "internal" purposes, like marketing, and for "external" purposes like licensing to others. There is a lot of cool stuff out there to exploit. And much of this cool content has value in monetary terms — thus the reason for calling it "currency" in this book. In fact, IP is increasingly seen around the globe as a significant and precious asset. IP accounts for more than 20 percent of world trade, which equals approximately US$740 billion.[1] Hopefully, this figure will entice you to begin thinking about what IP you own and how you can profit from it.

Since IBM introduced its personal computer (PC) in 1981 for use in the home, office, and schools, there has been a quiet proliferation of content or IP. Many people of all different backgrounds and experiences have been creating content for a variety of purposes, and in many cases they are not aware that the laws protect it, or that it is an asset which the marketplace will pay for.

People who used to spend their evenings or a rainy Sunday afternoon watching television now spend those same hours in front of their computers, searching the Internet, communicating with others, and creating their own content. They might create a family Web site, or scan into their computers vacation photographs to send to friends around the world, or write an article and try to sell it on the Internet. And with the proliferation of laptop computers, there is much "captured" time, whether in airports or coffeehouses, where people are pulling out their computers to create a work proposal or write a short story. There's an abundance of content available for distribution on the Internet.

Managing IP

There are three kinds of lies: lies, damned lies and statistics.

— Disraeli

Creating and owning IP is not enough. You need to determine its value, protect it from others, and know how to profit from it. Properly managing IP is the key to reaping substantial returns from it. And properly managing IP will be the distinguishing factor between those who benefit from their IP and those who do not. In other words, good ideas, proper packaging, and accessibility will lead to the content that will fill the Internet and the public's high and perhaps insatiable demand for quality "packaged" information.

This book is about recognizing your digital assets and profiting from them, an outcome that will derive from your decisions in managing your digital assets. You will soon have to ask yourself questions about whether you want to become a self-publisher and distributor of IP, whether you will license your IP for others to use, and how you will license it — to be used as-is or turned into value-added products. But first, what does it mean to properly manage IP? Are we talking business plans and corporate strategies? As someone who never went to business school, I take the simplest approach to organizing this information and call it the ABC approach.

The ABC Approach

Step A: You must first learn how to "count" digital assets, your IP. This includes IP created on your own, like a newsletter article or a travel photograph. And it includes works you've created for others and to which you've kept rights; for example, you may have written a report for a client who required the print rights but you've retained the rights to post that report on your Web site. You may have acquired other IP through licenses, such as the rights to include someone else's article in your book, or someone else's photograph on your Web site. Further, you may acquire IP through heredity (generally IP can be inherited just like furniture and money).

Pay careful attention to works you've created in employment and commissioned situations, as well as works jointly created, as you have to ensure that you have the rights to them. Such rights are often set out in a written agreement. If you have any written agreements regarding the ownership and licensing of IP, now is the time to dig them out and see what rights belong to you, what rights belong to the party with whom you made these agreements, and whether any rights revert back to you upon certain actions (such as writing a letter and "claiming" those rights), or after a certain period of time has elapsed.

In counting your digital assets, remember that a wealth of valuable content is needed for digital projects like Web sites and e-zines. Chances are you have already created some of that content, and are capable of creating much more of it. This may include course materials you prepared, business reports, articles for newsletters and other publications, databases, photographs, illustrations and designs, videos, sound recordings, and computer software programs. Although your child's drawings usually only have value to you and members of your family, there may be considerable value in a database of subscribers to your newsletter or your customer list.

Step B: Once you've counted your IP, you must estimate its value. This is a complicated task, and often you will have no concrete way to verify your estimates. As a brief summary, start by determining what has value and what doesn't. Then do some homework to see what others have paid for IP in similar situations. Then test the marketplace by trying to sell it. Pick a price with which you are comfortable, one that won't make you crack an obvious smile in a face-to-face meeting. Some of this pricing will of course be experimental but don't think of it as the price of your IP, think of it as the starting price for your negotiations. (Don't worry, there's a full chapter on "The Value of Digital Property.")

Step C: As a content creator and owner, you must always look towards the future. We now know that IP has value, but we are still figuring out how much value and to whom and in what form(s). It is likely that intangibles will have greater value in the future, whether it's because of the newer push technology on the Internet or people's frustrations with information overload. As an IP entrepreneur, you must always look for and discuss new ways to profit from your digital property.

Lastly, digital property is not static; it may be published on a CD-ROM today, tomorrow on the Internet, and next week, the same digital property may be licensed to someone else for further uses. The exploitation process of digital property is "alive" or ongoing. You must continuously be looking for ways to adapt your digital property for new uses — and new ways to profit.

The "Commercial" Internet

We are currently witnessing the growth of the Net from a non-commercial vehicle to a commercial one, at least in part. At one point in time, and this is still true but changing as I write this book, much of the content on the Net was accessible for free. But now we see segments of the Net where information is paid for, and we will continue to see more and more of this. From the perspective of the content owner, one important thing to be aware of is that people are willing to pay for certain content, but probably not for all content.

When auditing your IP, keep in mind that what the public won't pay for today, they may pay for tomorrow — if it's the right content, in the right format, at the right price. And if you want to promote your IP today so that it can be sold tomorrow, you might want to follow the examples of the many online publishers who have been making much of their content (mostly articles and other packaged information) available for free and are now beginning to sell more customized or selective or detailed content. The chapters on "Digital Property That Sells: Business Models on the Web" and "New Media Opportunities" describe various examples of online entrepreneurs and businesses which might stir you to think about your own opportunities in the online world.

In an effort to reconstruct and preserve the literary world from 1775 to 1850, the University of Virginia is creating computerized versions of about one-third of the American fiction published during the era. The project will digitally archive the enduring classics, as well as obscure books long out of print. . . . Some of the text will be released on the World Wide Web, but the whole collection will be sold to libraries on CD-ROM or be available on the Internet for a fee.[2]

What's interesting about the University of Virginia project is that a year or two earlier — the article appeared in January 1997 — people would probably have expected that the whole collection be released for free on the Web. Once again, we see evidence of change in the electronic world, our expectations, our values, and what constitutes a digital asset.

How Others Profit from Their Natural Resources

Below are a variety of examples of people and organizations who understand that their natural resources and digital assets have value — monetary value as well as promotional, educational, and possible future value.

Corporate Documents

Organizations have an abundance of materials that may be digital assets. In fact, organizations are beginning to digitize a variety of corporate records, including their logos, advertisements, annual reports, videos, photographs, graphic art and designs, trade show and seminar presentations, and employee and customer newsletters. This helps organize corporate documents which may otherwise be scattered among different departments of an organization, and it usually saves storage space. It also provides an opportunity to make use of the organization's original investment in creating those underlying works. Once digitized and compiled, with a system to efficiently access them, the works can be used again and again in further presentations and newsletters and Web sites, and in some circumstances portions or all of the records can be licensed or sold to others outside the organization.

As an example, Toronto-based Oshawa Group Ltd. put all of the photography from its annual reports from the past nine years on CD-ROM and now has a library of photos it can use for all sorts of purposes. As Tim Carter, vice president of public affairs for Oshawa Group, said about the cover of a recent company publication displaying a compilation of photographs, "We couldn't have done it if we hadn't digitized this because we needed a particular collection of photos, and we didn't have time to go through the hundreds and hundreds of photos we have to find them."[3]

More and more organizations are undertaking digitization projects that were not even contemplated a year or two ago.

Reuse of a Presentation

Whether created by an individual or an organization, there are examples on the Web of presentations and slide shows on a variety of subject matters. The value of these presentations is increased by making them continuously available, and keeping them updated, for anyone to access anytime and from anywhere.

Repurposed Works

As individuals realize that their day jobs often require them to create certain IP (like computer software), they are also becoming aware that that IP, or components of it, is valuable outside the workplace. One fellow I came across (who was careful not to infringe upon any ownership claims of his employer) began his own Web site where he now sells components and adapted versions of computer software developed at work. Other employees and consultants are publishing both short and long articles on the Web based on knowledge and experience gained from work. In certain circumstances, they also might be able to obtain nonexclusive rights to electronically publish articles and images that they originally created for their employers or clients.

Writings

There are many Web sites containing articles, poetry, and fiction, and in many instances these stories are accessible for free. However, in some the public must pay for the digitized stories. Some creators are selling and distributing their writings on their own Web sites, while others are employing the help of sites like The Story Store (*http://www.thestorystore.com/*), which is a nonfiction article clearinghouse for writers and editors. While allowing writers to display their works, The Story Store provides editors with an opportunity to purchase and download complete articles. Generally, the articles are intended for use in corporate newsletters and magazines, business and trade journals, and other periodicals. It operates on a consignment basis in that writers post their stories and are paid 60 percent of the sale price. The price of each article is based on word count and the complexity of the topic. Typical article prices range from US$75 for filler-type articles to US$500 for longer, more complex ones. Whether an author receives a byline is up to the purchasing editor. The editor may only use the story once, though additional use is possible for additional fees.

If you would like to take a look at some of the many electronic magazines or e-zines on the Internet, visit the Electronic Newsstand (*http://www.enews.com/*).

A Deal Is Struck

Many authors have been offered print book deals after establishing their presence on the Net, by offering a service or by publishing a work in part or whole. In early 1997, a major publishing house even signed an author based on a conversation that took place on the online service America Online (AOL). An editor from Simon and Schuster, who hosted a once-a-month hour-long "Ask the Editor" live chat on AOL's Book Central site, signed a twenty-something author to a two-book deal, for a significant six-figure sum.

Poets

The Web site Poetry World (*http://www.std.com/poetryworld/*) allows you to listen to live and prerecorded interviews with, and performances by, poets. The site also sells a variety of computer software, books, and audiotapes to help you create your own poems.

Serials and Soaps

Online soap operas, or cybersoaps, are a popular Internet form of entertainment. Using text, photographs, video, and audio, cybersoaps entice Web surfers to the same degree as the television soaps interest the TV-watching public. The Spot (*http://www.thespot.com/*), one of the earlier Internet soaps (now defunct), played out through daily entries in the digital diaries of the cast, a group of Generation Xers who shared a California beach house.

Bookselling

Simon and Schuster recently launched its Internet publishing site (*http://www.simonandschuster.com/*), offering an array of features such as subscription reference services and a chance to order books online. It also offers live author events, reader reviews, online newsletters, and bulletin boards.

At Canada's Virtual Bookstore (*http://www.cvbookstore.com/*), you can download an entire book. For Can$8.95, you'll receive a password by email to access this online book, but before downloading the book, you must agree to use the book for personal purposes only, by downloading it into your computer and/or printing it out, and not to otherwise reproduce it. Public domain titles have been available for downloading for many years in such places as Project Gutenberg (*http://www.promo.net/pg/*). Tara Publishing (*http://www.tarapublishing.com/*)has samplers of each of its many e-titles (mostly books), which can be downloaded and browsed for free. For literary Web surfers who want to see more online booksites, go to Bookwire (*http://www.bookwire.com/*), which lists hundreds of virtual booksellers, as well as the Complete Guide to Online Bookstores (*http://www.paperz.com /bookstores.html*).

In four weekly installments which began January 16, 1997, Music Central (*http://musiccentral.msn.com/*) aired an online serialization of a book by Fred Goodman, in a deal between the Microsoft Network and Times Books, a division of Random House Inc.

Builder Online (*http://www.builderonline.com/*) has a variety of IP for sale in its online store, including house plans, seminars, books, magazines, reprints of articles, CD-ROMs, tapes, and workbooks.

Customized Publishing

The Internet is a wonderful tool for customized publishing. For instance, if you're a teacher pulling together materials for your class from various sources, instead of leaving a lengthy reading list at the library, you can now publish your own choice of reading selections. For an example of one custom publisher, see McGraw-Hill's Primis Custom Publishing site (*http://www.mhhe.com/primis/*).

Also, with digital publishing, publishing-on-demand becomes viable. Publishers do not need to print huge numbers of books, keep them in stock, and ship them out. A publisher can now respond to each individual order from a customer and electronically deliver the "goods" within seconds of the request. It is likely that publishing-on-demand will become more popular.

Audio and Audiovisual E-Publishing

Many people think of electronic publishing or e-publishing as text-based publishing. But sheet music, photographs, art and images, recorded interviews and music, as well as video clips, are all IP we're seeing displayed, sold, and distributed via the Internet.

EMI Music Publishing's library music division, KPM Music, provides an online archive and distribution system for copyright owners of music (*http://www.software.ibm.com/is/dig-lib/dlemi.htm*). You can search for different types of music in the library, listen to sample recordings slightly downgraded in quality, choose what you want to purchase, fill out an online rights clearance form, and immediately download and use professional-quality music. The archive is specifically designed for filmmakers, broadcasters, and advertising agencies who require music for their productions.

A popular online music store is CDnow (*http://www.cdnow.com/*). In addition to containing more than 150,000 titles, which can be shipped within one day anywhere in North America, CD now lets you listen to thousands of tunes. It also publishes music news and album chart listings and has a jukebox that can play music while you browse. Other online music stores are ABCDs (*http://www.abcds.com/*) and CDworld (*http://www.cdworld.com/*).

Further, various radio and television broadcasters use the Web to publish manuscripts from interviews and programs as well as audio and video files, with links to similar stories or related information on the Web. You can view a video clip of a hockey game, for example, from the Web site of the Canadian Broadcasting Corporation (CBC) (*http://www.cbc.ca/*).

Maps

In certain businesses, maps of districts, cities, countries, and so on are used on a daily basis. These maps originate from both government and private sources. Once digitized, these maps can have tremendous benefits as they can quickly be printed on demand and easily adapted to meet a variety of purposes. For example, they can be used in information kiosks for tourists, for sophisticated Geographical Information Systems (GIS), and for personal and business travel purposes.

For a map example, see MapQuest (*http://www.mapquest.com/*), a subsidiary of GeoSystems Global Corporation. GeoSystems has been selling digital mapping systems for five years to CD-ROM publishers and companies that offer operator-assisted services to cellphone users, as well as the American Automobile Association. Although MapQuest currently offers many of its "goods" for free on the Web, it has two ways in which it plans to make money from digitized maps. One is by selling advertisements at two cents per page viewed. At the time of writing, MapQuest claims 100,000 daily visitors to its Web site. Additional advertising fees (double the rate) are available for those who want geographical targeting — a hotel, for instance, which may want its ad to appear whenever someone makes an online request for a route map near that hotel. The other revenue source is from selling its IP or maps directly to Web site owners, such as real estate agents, retail chains, travel agencies or restaurants. Fees, ranging from US$2,500 to $30,000 a year, are based on the number of maps and allow the licensee to repackage the maps as their own. For example, MapQuest recently began providing interactive mapping content to the Sabre Group, Inc., for its popular Travelocity Web site (*http://www.travelocity.com/*).

In addition, MapQuest already has one million registered users who may download maps of their home or office location, adapt them by adding further information, and forward them to others. Lastly, MapQuest is exploiting new revenue sources by asking users to pay them directly for the use of maps, or by asking hotels and airlines to pay them a commission for business brought to them because of MapQuest.

Kiosks

Although recipes for food are generally not protected by copyright, recipes are content that may have value in the digital world. In 1995 when I was living in Los Angeles, I frequented a grocery store that had a "recipe kiosk." All I had to do was punch in a type of recipe or kind of food and a selection of recipes would appear onscreen that could be printed out. For many, this was a wonderful convenience that meant all the necessary ingredients could be purchased in a single shopping trip without any recipe homework prior to heading to the grocery store.

Kiosks with information for tourists about restaurants, hotels, and local attractions are becoming more popular.

Libraries

Libraries are digitizing their collections. That doesn't mean they are digitizing the printed books and magazines they loan out, as it is unlikely that libraries own the IP in these books and magazines — they may have the right to loan them to the public but not to reproduce them without the permission of their authors or publishers. But similar to museums and archives, libraries have a wealth of content that would be more easily accessible and therefore more valuable to the public if it were in a digital format. Some interesting projects by libraries include the following.

The Denver Public Library in Denver, Colorado, is digitizing its History of the American West, 1860–1920, collection. The finished project will include 7,500 photos documenting the lives of the Plains, Mountain, and Southwestern tribes of Native Americans and the mining booms in Colorado, as well as access to 48,000 previously digitized images in the Denver Western History Collection.

The Ohio Historical Society in Columbus, Ohio, is digitizing its collection on The African-American Experience in Ohio, 1850–1920. A collection of 22,000 pages of text and images will be digitized, focusing on issues like slavery and emancipation, religion, public opinion, and political action.

A collection of American Environmental Photographs, 1897–1931, is being digitized by the University of Chicago, in Chicago, Illinois. The digitized project will include 5,800 photographic images depicting natural environments and ecological plant communities in their original state throughout the United States.

A collection of 8,241 photographs of northeastern Mexico and the South Texas border area, entitled The South Texas Border,

1900–1920, with images of the diverse ethnic groups living in the communities, military preparation for the Mexican Revolution and World War I, and the natural and built environment, is being digitized by the University of Texas, in Austin, Texas.

The George Bush Digital Library, which consists of over 36 million pages of documents, 1.5 million photographs, 6,000 hours of audio/video, and 40,000 museum artifacts, is being digitized for use on the Internet. The project is a collaboration between Texas A&M University in College Station, Texas, and the U.S. National Archives and Records Administration.

One of the larger library digitization projects is at the Archivo General de Indias, in Seville, Spain. This archive houses the most important documents on the discovery, exploration, and administration of the Americas by the Spaniards. More than nine million pages have been scanned into this digital library.

Virtual Libraries

In addition to working on specific digitization projects, many libraries are becoming online or virtual libraries, by making materials and services available to the public via the Internet or other online methods. Services might include providing information about the community related to recreation, geography, politics, taxes, or local businesses. If there is a large Asian population in the community, for instance, the library might include information specifically geared to that community as well as links to other helpful Web sites. Or perhaps the virtual library will offer information for teens or seniors. There might be information about the library itself, how to access the collection, how to reserve and renew library materials online, or how to use the Internet for library purposes. And the virtual library might promote local writers, have audio recordings of readings, or list writing courses and author events.

There are various virtual libraries on the Internet. One example is the Richmond Public Library in British Columbia (*http://www*

.rpl.richmond.bc.ca/). The Canadian Initiative on Digital Libraries (*http://www.nlc-bnc.ca/cidl/*) has interesting resources and information on digital libraries.

Your Own Library

The interesting notion about a digital library is that individuals may begin to have their own private libraries. For instance, just as you can publish a magazine on your Web site, you could make materials you've collected from research — including text, images, audio, and video — available to certain people, or to the public at large.

Digitized Art

> *The art world, never allergic to a social trend and recovering from the bust that followed the market boom of the 1980s, has been quietly but intently gravitating to that gravityless, giddy boom town in cyberspace called the World Wide Web, where text and pictures are easily displayed on what are known as sites or pages.*
>
> — Steven Henry Madoff, *New York Times*[4]

The licensing of IP is not new to museums. We've all purchased postcards, posters, and books from museum gift shops. Perhaps you were one of the visitors to the famed Matisse show at the Museum of Modern Art (MOMA) in New York in 1993 and contributed to the US$25 million in merchandising revenues for MOMA that year. Look at the strength of that one exhibit — merchandising revenues were $16 million the year before and $18 million the subsequent year.

Although much of the museum merchandising we currently see is in the form of posters, postcards, mugs, T-shirts, and other clothing items, we are now seeing museums and galleries digitize their collections. For instance, a museum might digitize its Inuit art collection so that others can use the digitized images on their

Web sites or in a CD-ROM. Museums have vast quantities of works which can be digitized — valuable content when packaged in the right form. It is likely that we will see museums and art galleries put more effort into licensing their digital images, which can earn both money and a wider reputation for their institutions and the works in their collections.

Bill Gates's company Corbis (*http://www.corbis.com/*) obtains licenses from photographers, museums, and archives around the world to use their digitized images. Corbis uses the digitized images for its own purposes, including in CD-ROMs it has produced, and it licenses the rights to other companies for use in CD-ROMs and other digital products, and to new media producers, print publishers, art directors, designers, and other communications professionals. Other players in the digital image market include West Stock Photography (*http://www.weststock.com/*), PhotoDisc (*http://www.photodisc.com/*), and Picture Network International (*http://www.publishersdepot.com/*).

In addition, individual artists are opening their own online galleries to display and sell their art. By surfing the Web, you can visit many of these galleries.

With the ever expanding Internet, it is difficult to guess the size of the virtual-art market. However, from July through November 1995, 4,850 artists, museums, galleries, and other arts organizations around the globe listed visual-arts sites in the Yahoo! directory (*http://www.yahoo.com/*), a popular search engine or index to the Internet.

Museum Projects

There are a variety of digitization projects being undertaken in museums around the world. Some interesting examples of projects, created for various purposes and end users, are set out below.

The goal of one of the projects of the National Archives of Canada (*http://www.archives.ca/*) is to scan 28,000 caricatures, 14,000 nitrate images from the Karsh photograph collection,

3,000 images from the color transparency collection, and 25,000 stamp images from the Postal Archives. This information will then be available through the Internet.

Canada's Visual History/Histoire du Canada en Images (CD-ROM), a project of the federal government's Canadian Heritage Information Network (*http://www.chin.gc.ca/*), is aimed at secondary school and college students. The CD-ROM will compile recent research with images not generally accessible to students and teachers, including 2,400 paintings, drawings, maps, and charts from the collections of archives, libraries, and museums throughout Canada.

The Canadian Museum of Nature is working on an interactive CD-ROM project, Arctic Journey, for use by schools, libraries, and the home computer market. The product will contain information about the people, art, music, explorations, scientific research, flora and fauna, landscape, and economy of the North.

The Canadian Museum of Civilization (*http://www.civilization.ca/*) is involved in a project of digitizing up to 6,000 images of native artifacts from its analog collection. Parks Canada (*http://pks-intrnet-www.pch.gc.ca/*) is preparing the electronic version of its National Parks System Plan Book.

The descriptions of these projects do not say whether "consumers" will be charged to use them. It is likely that some uses will be for free and others paid for. What all this "digital" activity indicates is that there are a lot of natural resources that have a lot of value to people, and many institutions and governments are showing their commitment by allocating budgets to these projects because they believe that they are valuable to society. Although profit is one reason for museums to digitize their collections, also important is the publicity gained from having a presence on the Net and the opportunity it provides for continuing to inform and educate the public.

In fact, there are more and more governments and businesses displaying and selling their digitized documents on the Internet. Why not sell yours?

Final Word

Start your own digitization projects by examining your natural resources. Consider what digital assets you own, what their value is, and what potential uses and markets exist. Examples of digitization projects in this chapter and throughout the book may inspire you to consider undertaking projects to take advantage of your digital assets. Chapter 3 looks at projects undertaken by people who were specifically seeking to earn revenue from them and examines the business models new media entrepreneurs use for their digital-based enterprises.

End Notes

1. Stacy Snowman, "Conducting Intellectual Property Audits 1996," 429 PLI/Pat 7 at 9.

2. "Rare Books Digitally Scanned," *Globe and Mail,* 4 January 1997, p. C12.

3. Tim Carter, quoted in Janet McFarland, "Photographer Takes Shot at Multimedia," *Globe and Mail,* 2 December 1996, p. B7.

4. Steven Henry Madoff, "Art in Cyberspace: Can It Live without a Body," *New York Times,* 21 January 1996, sec. 2, p. 1.

P A R T 2

Currency of the
Twenty-First Century

CHAPTER 3
Digital Property That Sells:
Business Models on the Web

It's not what I do, but the way I do it.
It's not what I say, but the way I say it.

— Mae West

While there is an abundance of content in digital form, generated by digital means, or capable of being digitized, the value of that digital property varies from non-revenue generating (that is, its value lies in advertising other products and services) to "direct" value (for example, selling digital property for a fixed dollar amount). What's consistently evident is that digital property is increasingly becoming more valuable and has greater potential as a "product" to be sold on the Internet. More and more digital property is being sold on the Net through a variety and combination of means. Many of these efforts are in the experimental stage. And we are already seeing certain ventures that failed in their initial attempts to sell digital property on the Net but, rather than abandoning the idea, are now trying alternative approaches. This chapter examines some of the business models and strategies employed for selling IP on the Internet.[1]

What's Selling Online

> *There is no reason anyone would want a computer in their home.*
>
> — Ken Olson, founder and former president of Digital Equipment, in 1977

The most common online purchases are for computer software, music recordings, and travel services.[2] Books and magazines are also frequently purchased from the Web. It's no coincidence that the most common online transactions include IP. Because of IP's very nature (and its ease of digitization), it can be easily bought and sold through an online or Net transaction, and equally important, it can be delivered online. Plus, choosing IP from an online store is intimidation-free — there's no sales pressure, for example, when you listen to a music recording on the Internet before purchasing it rather than actually browsing through a physical music store. The selection in an online store can be very large since the merchandise is stored in digital form and not in a large warehouse. Lastly, consumers are more comfortable making purchases on the Internet for relatively small dollar amounts (which is usually the situation when buying IP), a comfort factor which is extremely important in the infancy of electronic commerce.

Business Models on the Web

Seven business models for online transactions — subscription, consignment, commission, revenue-sharing, flat fee, advertising, transaction fee, and pay-per-use — are described below.

➧ **Subscription model:** This model consists of a time-based payment for a regular product or service, such as an annual subscription to an e-zine. This is akin to the magazine publishing or cable television model. In this situation, the customer/subscriber pays an annual fee for access to the e-zine and the electronic publisher earns its revenue from that subscription fee. (Often the publisher also earns revenue from selling advertising space in the magazine, or time on cable television. The advertising model is discussed below.)

As of February 1997, half of the largest circulation print magazines in the United States had Web sites and many others were at the planning stage. Much of the content on these Web sites is available for free but this is starting to change. For instance, *Barron's*, a well-known U.S. financial magazine that began publishing a free online edition (*http://www.barrons.com/*), now makes the online version available exclusively to subscribers of another online magazine, the *Wall Street Journal Interactive Edition* (*http://www.wsj.com/*). Launched in April 1996 on a five-month *free* trial, the *WSJ Interactive Edition* attracted 650,000 nonpaying subscribers. It was relaunched in September 1996 on a paid subscription basis, and the number of paying subscribers dropped to 30,000 (40 percent of whom were also print subscribers). The cost is US$29 per year for print subscribers (in addition to the print subscription price of US$175), or US$49 per year for nonprint subscribers.

Print publishers that have gone online generally derive revenue from a variety of sources, including subscriber fees, advertising, fees for the use of archived newspapers (either digital archives or print versions), licensing fees from an arrangement with an online service for the use of their publication by the service's subscribers, and a personalized news service that charges transaction fees. These business models are discussed below. If you want to take a look at how some of these models work on the Web, see *Mercury Center* (*http://www.sjmercury.com/*) and ESPNet SportsZone (*http://espnet.sportszone.com/*).

For e-publishers who do not have a print publication, there may be even more unknowns as their product has not before been tested in the print environment. An illustration of an e-zine that has dropped its subscriber fees is *Slate* (*http://www.slate.com/*), Microsoft's online political magazine. As of August 1997, *Slate* was not charging for the magazine but may charge for it once again in the future. (*Slate* does charge a fee, however, to mail a hard copy of the magazine to a very small group of traditional subscribers.) Comparably, the online version of *USA Today* (*http:// www.usatoday.com/*) attempted a US$12.95 per month access fee, but eliminated the fee because of lack of subscriber interest. Although it seems that subscribers will pay for information, they will not pay for all information and are most likely to pay for very timely, specific, personalized information.

Free Content

One trend that is emerging in online publishing is providing certain content for free while charging for enhanced services or more detailed content. This way consumers can sample the content available from the e-publisher and choose to pay for specific content on a case-by-case basis. For the e-publisher, it is a method of obtaining ongoing feedback from consumers about the content they are interested in and willing to pay for. It is also a means of continuously advertising their paid products.

David Talbot, editor and CEO of *Salon* (*http://www.salon1999.com/*), an online magazine with no print version, is an optimistic publisher and asserts that people will pay subscriber fees for enhanced services like chat sessions with well-known authors, writers' workshops, and discounts at certain bookstores. *Salon* was launched in November 1995, though at the time of writing this book, Talbot had not undertaken any market research to prove his point, nor does *Salon* require payments to access the content on its Web site. If subscriber fees become a reality for *Salon*, but do not work, Talbot says that *Salon* may venture into producing specialized content through multiple channels and having a further presence on the Web that focuses on such things as women's issues, food, and travel. Some of *Salon*'s competitors are *Slate* (*http://www.slate.com/*), *Feed* (*http://www.feedmag.com/*), and *Suck* (*http://www.suck.com/*).

Disney

Disney recently launched its first fee-charging online venture. As of April 1997, for US$4.95 per month, anyone can have access through Disney's Web site (*http://www.disneyblast.com/*) to games, puzzles, and stories featuring Mickey, Donald, Goofy, and their friends. The site also contains an ABC News report prepared for children and sports scores and highlights from the ESPN sports network.

In addition to subscriber fees, Disney sells advertising on its Web site, and has entered into an exclusive arrangement with the online service MSN (Microsoft Network) by which Disney earns additional money by providing content. MSN subscribers do not have to pay Disney's monthly subscriber fee to access Disney's Daily Blast. Disney understands that subscriber fees have not been overly welcome on the Net; however, it feels that it has a leg up on others because of its unique properties and IP. Further, Disney feels that other Web sites that are charging subscribers are not providing original content but are merely including articles and other works that appear in, for instance, a print version of a magazine. Disney projects that it will attract subscribers by offering "new" content and not merely a digital version of a print magazine.

➡ **Consignment model:** This works like any consignment relationship. In this situation, a content owner might post her works on someone else's Web site. When the Web site "sells" the work, the content owner would then be entitled to a percentage of the sale price. This is often how an artist earns income, by displaying his work in an art gallery on consignment.

The Story Store (*http://www.thestorystore.com/*), which was discussed in the previous chapter, is a consignment example. It is a nonfiction article clearinghouse for writers and editors. Writers display their works on The Story Store Web site for editors to examine and purchase. If the articles are sold, writers are paid 60 percent of the sale price. The price of each article is based on word count and the complexity of the topic, and it typically ranges from US$75 for filler-type articles to US$500 for longer ones. The editor may only use the story once, though additional use is possible for additional fees.

➡ **Commission model:** This model entitles an individual or company that sells a product or service on behalf of another individual or company to a commission (a percentage of the revenue).

PictureVision, Inc. (*http://www.picturevision.com/*), which stores online copies of customers' photographs (see details in chapter 7), is entitled to a portion of the money earned from various transactions in which it is involved. For instance, when a customer pays $5 to have a roll of film digitized and stored online at the PhotoNet site, PictureVision gets 50–60 cents from the development lab (which is approximately twice the amount it costs PictureVision to provide the necessary fifteen megabytes of disk space for a month). When customers order reprints or other products like greetings cards, mugs, and T-shirts with photos on them, PictureVision gets a percentage of the monies earned from the company that actually supplies the end product to the customer. Further, software publishers like Microsoft and Adobe have incorporated links to the PhotoNet site into their photo-editing packages so their consumers can download pictures from the Net and manipulate them. These software publishers pay PictureVision for this use, and then receive a commission every time a user pays to download a photo.

➡ **Revenue-sharing with online services model:** This describes an arrangement between a content/IP owner and an online service like AOL, CompuServe, or MSN whereby the content/IP owner shares in the revenue earned from subscribers to the online service.

For example, if a subscriber to an online service pays $1.00 an hour for time spent in an online news site, the online service might retain 75 percent of that amount and submit 25 percent of the amount earned to the content owner.

One online service, which charges consumers a fixed monthly amount for unlimited access, pays content owners a flat fee for "unique and compelling" content which is offered to consumers as part of the service, without additional charge. However, in circumstances where the provider charges both subscription and hourly fees (e.g., for use of the online service in certain countries), the provider pays certain content owners a percentage of the average hourly usage revenues collected when consumers use that particular content.

Note that some online services are only interested in entering deals with established businesses with proven track records, and it may be difficult for less-established new media entrepreneurs and content owners to enter into concrete relationships with them.

➡ **Flat fee model:** This includes Web sites that provide some free content, and that charge fees for access to certain specialized portions of the site.

For a flat monthly or yearly fee, subscribers to the ESPN Sports-Zone Web site (*http://espnet.sportszone.com/*) receive breaking news stories, sports highlights, and scores, as well as access to expert columnists, cutting-edge graphics, player profiles, multimedia containing "best dunks, homers and touchdowns," and a sports almanac.

➡ **Advertising model:** This popular model involves charging fees for advertising on a Web site. The typical online ad is a banner that appears at the top or side of a Web page and is a hyperlink that the consumer can click on to visit the advertiser's Web site.

Online advertising has some unique features that set it apart from traditional advertising. For instance, it can be interactive and allow for two-way communication between the consumer and advertiser. It can also target audiences more specifically.

In 1996, advertising rates for the top Web sites ranged from US$15,000 to $100,000 per quarter. Web advertising is rapidly growing, at a rate of 50 percent per year in dollar terms. In 1995, US$50 million was earned from Web advertising, which can be compared to the US$180 billion for the entire U.S. advertising industry. Note that the top ten Web advertisers accounted for approximately 75 percent of all advertising revenue; these top advertisers include computer software companies, online services, online publishers, and travel companies. Most advertising revenue was generated through Web sites for Internet search engines and computer software for navigating or surfing the Web.

Generally, print newspapers earn 30 percent of their revenue, and magazines 40 to 60 percent of their revenue, from subscriptions, and the remainder of their income is earned from advertising. Judging by current perceptions of subscriber fees on the Net, advertising may be the major source of revenue for online publications for quite a while — but only time will tell!

For examples of advertising models, see Pathfinder (the Time Warner site created in October 1994) (*http://www.pathfinder.com/*), *Wall Street Journal Interactive Edition* (*http://www.wsj.com/*), and Yahoo! (*http://www.yahoo.com/*). On these and other Web sites, you will find various versions of advertising, primarily in the form of "banners" or rectangles advertising products and services. By clicking on the banners, the Web surfer or consumer is guided to another Web site with more detailed information about the product or service. Yahoo!, one of the most popular search engines on the Net, earned US$9.5 million in first-quarter sales in 1997 from advertisers.

Pathfinder earns US$2.5 million a year in advertising revenue and recently entered into an arrangement with the online service CompuServe, worth an additional US$3.5 million a year, to provide its *Personal Edition*, a personalized distillation of *Time, Sports Illustrated, Money*, and other Time Warner publications. However, it has not yet made any profit, as it costs US$10 million a year to support Pathfinder and its staff of seventy people. Even though Pathfinder has about three million visitors a week, which makes it one of the most popular Web sites, Time Warner feels that it takes a new medium five to seven years to become profitable.

An alternative to banner advertising on the Web can be seen at Mind's Eye Fiction (*http://tale.com/*), where an advertiser is asked to sponsor a short story so that the reader of the story does not have to pay to read it. The advertiser only has to pay if the reader accesses and interacts with the Web page of the advertiser. The interaction can be listening to an audio clip or watching a video, taking a customer survey, playing a game, doing a quiz, or browsing a catalog. The site "encourages" readers to interact with the ads by withholding the story's ending — to finish the story, readers must either participate in the ad or pay a fee.

Another alternative to banner advertisements is classified ads. For example, *Reunions Magazine* (*http://www.execpc.com/~reunions/*) sells its classified ads, which have a large audience, for US$1 per word per month. *The Dog Zone* (*http://www.dogzone.com/*) generates revenue from both its banner ads and classified ads. Classified advertisements range from US$15 to $25 per month, depending on their length. Banner ads (usually from kennels and dog equipment suppliers) cost approximately US$300 per month. The classified advertisements also include a "lost dog" section, where listings are free.

Notwithstanding some of the successful Web advertising stories, advertisers do not yet have sufficient information to determine how well their advertisements are doing on the Net, or to make comparisons with their advertising dollars spent on TV, print, or direct mail.

Advertising rates for the Internet are much lower than for other media, partly because it is a new medium and there are many unknowns. People "trust" established media like newspapers, radio, and television. In time, the same will be true of the Internet. In fact, when television was introduced to the public, people were surprised at how quickly advertisers were willing to pay big bucks for advertising!

➡ **Transaction fee model:** This includes purchasing products and services through a Web site. For example, a book, music recording, plans for building a shed or boat, or part of a database could be purchased from a Web site, and often immediately delivered to the customer in a digital form on the Internet.

Web sites can be online stores where products and services are bought and sold. However, to date, Web sites have not merely been stores, they have also been providers of much "free" content or "value-added" services. The "value-added" portions include anything from additional information on a certain topic to inter-active communication to audio and video works. For example, Amazon.com (*http://www.amazon.com/*), a Seattle-based online bookstore, provides its customers with a monthly email informing them of new books on topics they choose. Amazon.com is one of the greatest success stories on the Internet due to the amount of books it has sold through its Web site, and it has provided inspiration for many new media entrepreneurs. Books have been ordered online from over sixty-six countries.

Online music stores are quickly becoming popular. They often allow customers to preview, order, pay-per-listen, and download music, and at the same time they ensure that owners of the IP can control their works and be paid for them. See, for example, CDnow (*http://cdnow.com/*), ABCDs (*http://www.abcds.com/*), Global Electronic Music Marketplace (*http://gemm.com*), and CDworld (*http://www.cdworld.com/*).

→ **Pay-per-use model:** Also known as "software metering," this model allows a consumer to pay for digital property based on her use of it. This would allow a consumer to access digital property like computer software, a database, or an electronic book on the Internet and pay for the portions she downloads or amount of time she uses it while online.

Software metering can be particularly advantageous for a consumer or business who only requires use of a portion of a digital work. For example, a person could access a list of librarians in the United Kingdom from a larger database of librarians around the world, or a list of computer software publishers in the state of California from a list of U.S. software publishers. The user would only pay for that portion of the database, as opposed to paying for the entire database.

It is likely that this method would be popular with people who use some of the larger, more expensive databases (and databases can be quite expensive!). For the owner of the database, it means new revenue from consumers who only need to use a small portion of a database and may otherwise not purchase it. It may also be an appropriate business model for computer games that have a short shelf life, for "limited-use" software that you might use only once (such as the yearly updated program you use to prepare your income tax return), or to access a chapter or two from a book.

Variations on this model might include paying per "bit." In other words, a consumer would pay for the amount of time she listens to online music, or for the resolution of a photograph.

Collecting Payment for Online Purchases

> *The old game was about having unique data or recognized leadership in filtering data. In the new game, the instant accessibility and usability of that information will be even more important.*
>
> — Michael Treacy, *Globe and Mail*[3]

If you sell your digital property on the Internet, you will have to consider how to collect payment for it. Some new media entrepreneurs are collecting money offline, which means purchasers must mail their check or credit card information or place the order by telephone, while others provide for online payment.

One unique payment consideration for owners of digital property is that much of the property can be sold at extremely small prices, say ten cents for a newspaper article or five cents for a photograph, or less. Because of this, microcommerce or micropayment systems have developed to allow the buying and selling of content on the Internet for as little as fractions of a cent, referred to as "microtransactions" in online parlance. These systems use electronic cash or ecash. They are ideal for content creators and owners who sell text, images, film clips, music, games, and computer software.

There are various micropayment systems. One model allows the consumer to purchase a "wallet" pre-loaded with ecash equivalent to, let's say, five dollars, which he would spend over a period of time by buying an article here for two cents, an audio clip there for five cents, an image for one cent, and so on. Some microcommerce systems are designed to support Web transactions from as small as one-tenth of a cent up to five dollars, which may be suitable for content owners selling articles, cartoons by the strip, and individual songs.

Micropayment systems include Millicent, at Digital Equipment Corporation (*http://www.research.digital.com/SRC/millicent/*), First Virtual (*http://www.fv.com/*), CyberCash (*http://www.cybercash.com/*), NetBill Project (*http://www.netbill.com/*), and DigiCash (*http://www.digicash.com/*).

At the time of writing this book, online payments for microtransactions are still getting their feet wet. One system, Cyber-Cash, has signed up only eight hundred online merchants to its system after nearly two years of trying.[4] As content owners provide more valuable content on the Net, and as consumers become more willing to pay for that content, especially at the reasonable prices that are feasible through these micropayment systems, these systems are likely to become a popular payment scheme for buying and selling digital property on the Internet. And considering the US$500 million worth of business taking placing on the Internet in 1996 (according to Forrester Research, a Boston-based technology research and consulting firm specializing in the Internet), it is likely that fewer and fewer purchases will be credit card transactions and more and more will be through ecash.

➡ **Statutory regulations:** Payment for certain content may be subject to statutory regulation. For instance, the public performance of music may be subject to a fee set by a quasi-judicial body.

An interesting development to watch for relates to the use of music on the Internet. On September 29, 1995, the Society of Composers, Authors and Music Publishers of Canada (SOCAN) (*http://www.socan.ca/*) filed with the Canadian Copyright Board their statement of proposed royalties to be collected for the use of music on computer online services, electronic bulletin board services, and, more generally, on the Internet. The proposed tariff is sometimes referred to as the "Internet Tariff." At the time of writing this book, the Canadian Copyright Board is going through proceedings with the affected and interested parties to determine whether this tariff will be set by the board, and if so, what its scope will be.

➡ **Copyright collectives and rights agencies:** In some situations, IP owners permit a collective or agency to license their works on their behalf. The collective or agency enters into the proper arrangements with the consumer, collects the royalties or payments due, and distributes the collected monies to the IP owners.

This is the model used for collecting payment for the public performance of music around the world. In the United States, ASCAP (*http://www.ascap.com/*) and BMI (*http://www.bmi.com/*) collect the payments. With ASCAP and BMI, royalty payments are transparent. Every time you hear music being played in a public place like a bar or concert hall or on television, the rights holder of that music is being paid. These and other similar organizations around the world have acted as models for groups that now collect payments for other types of copyright-protected works, such as photocopying fees for print books and magazines.

Rights collectives and agencies for electronic uses have begun to form and to collect royalties for the use of texts and images on the Internet. It is likely that the role of these collectives and agencies will quickly expand as they have for the performing rights in music and for photocopying text. One such agency is the Authors Registry (*http://www.webcom.com/registry/main.html*), a not-for-profit organization formed in May 1995.

Final Word

The various business models described in this chapter can work individually or in combination with one another, and the examples above show that many different organizations are attempting to earn revenues from the Internet. As a creator or owner of content, you can open your own "digital shop" on the Internet using one or a combination of these business models, or you may choose to enter into an arrangement with one of the individuals or businesses who already have a presence on the Internet. However you proceed, you must determine at what price to sell or license your IP to your potential customers. The next chapter deals with how to value, or put a price tag on, your IP.

End Notes

1. This chapter focuses on online models and strategies for selling IP. There are, of course, many other methods of selling digital property such as on computer disks and CD-ROMs. However, online transactions are already taking the lead in sales of digital property.

2. Salem Alaton, "Mining the Internet," *Globe and Mail*, 17 December 1996, p. B27.

3. Michael Treacy, "What's Driving the Information Shakeup," *Globe and Mail*, 6 June 1997, p. B10.

4. Tim Jackson, "Dawn of Micro-Payment Era," *Financial Times* [London], 26 May 1997, p. 17.

CHAPTER 4

The Value of Digital Property

No man but a blockhead ever wrote, except for money.

— Samuel Johnson (quoting a college tutor)

Not everyone agrees with the premise that IP has a monetary value on the Internet and in other digital forms. In fact, some think that all information on the Net should be available for free, a topic which could be the subject of its own book. That being said, this is a practical chapter. It attempts to put a price tag on your IP, an extremely tricky area since the only value of IP is what someone will pay for it. This chapter provides some guidance on setting the value of IP in the current as well as in the future marketplace.

The Worldwide Value of IP

IP is increasingly being viewed as an important and valuable asset around the world. As mentioned earlier, IP accounts for more than 20 percent of world trade, which equals approximately US$740 billion.[1] This worldwide figure manifests the significance of determining the value of your own IP.

Does Information Have Value?

You must take into account all of the surrounding circumstances when valuing your IP. As previously explained, the valuable ele-

ment in information may be the way in which it is packaged, filtered, customized, and enhanced. Its value may also lie in the
speed at which it can be accessed in that filtered mode, or in the
presence of an index to help users journey through specific portions of it (including via interactivity). The presence or absence
of competitors in the marketplace offering a similar product will
affect the value of your IP. Authenticity of the content is also
important. With the vast quantities of content on the Internet
supplied by a variety of people and organizations, packaged
information that is accurate and reliable will have greater value
than other information.

*Always keep in mind that people do not want to pay for more infor-
mation; they want to pay for less of it. The quicker they can turn
that information into value at work or home, the more valuable the
information.*

Further, if you offer a unique product, people will pay for it.
Stated another way, people want personalized information. The
relatively new services using "push" technology to deliver customized information packages are rapidly gaining popularity.
Push technology means that the content you want is delivered,
or "pushed," directly to your computer screen or to your email
address, as opposed to "pull" technology where you must go into
the relevant Web site and "pull" the required content for yourself. These services provide new or "newsworthy" content from
the Web covering certain topics as requested by the consumer.
Some of these customized services are available for a fee (see
chapter 3, "Digital Property That Sells"), which shows that
people are willing to pay for information, some of which may
already be available for free, because of the way in which it is filtered, packaged, and made available to them.

Where Is the Value?

Before you can place a price tag on IP, you must recognize where
its value comes from. At the root of this value are the character-

istics that distinguish IP from tangible property. Because IP can be simultaneously consumed by more than one consumer (e.g., computer software, a Web site, or a sound recording can be used by many people at the same time, unlike a car or a piece of jewelry), its value in many (although not all) respects lies in its ability to be multiplied in identical copies. Therefore, you cannot always place an economic value on a single piece of computer software or a book or digital photograph by looking at it as a single product; rather, you must evaluate the rights in the particular IP that are capable of being duplicated, so that the product can be used by many consumers simultaneously in many different forms and media.

The same is true, and at the same time untrue, with respect to other types of IP. For instance, a painting is a unique, one-of-a-kind work. At the same time, however, even though there is much value in the original work, there is also much value in multiple copies of it, in the form of art posters and digitized images, for example.

We will return many times to the concept of "rights" in IP and to the relevance of various media, including digital media, which relates directly to the value of IP. Books, for example, which until recently only had value in print form, now have value in digital form (e.g., on the Internet), and they may have value in other digital forms which we don't even know about yet. These known and unknown forms must all be accounted for when valuing IP.

Who Will Use Your IP and How?

In determining the value of your IP, consider both the licensee (the person or organization to whom you are licensing your digital property) and the purpose to which your IP will be put. You may be licensing your IP to a developer/producer/publisher creating a digital encyclopedia, or to a consumer/end-user who wants to use an image on the Web site where he sells his comic strips. You may be licensing your IP to a nonprofit organization or to a large commercial organization. These different licensees will have different perspectives on the value of your IP. The developer may look at your IP as "raw material," as an investment in the development of a digital product, and as a business expense. An organization might use your IP on a Web site or on the cover of its annual report. As the owner of IP, you may be able to license the same digital property to a developer and to an organization at the same or different times for the same or different prices. Each use has its own value.

Dollar Amount

Some rock 'n' roll fans sneered when they learned last week that the bad-boy Rolling Stones had sold their tunes to an advertiser. Microsoft bought "Start Me Up" to launch Windows 95, paying about $4 million.

— Kevin Goldman, *Wall Street Journal*[2]

Wouldn't it be wonderful if all of us could sell our IP to Microsoft for $4 million, or even $1 million, or even for $1,000. On the other hand, let's look at why Microsoft paid this hefty amount for the "Start Me Up" tune by the Rolling Stones. Basically, the Stones have valuable, internationally recognized property. Lesson to be learned: IP can have tremendous value in the right circumstances. Also, keep in mind that the Stones probably couldn't sell their IP at the beginning of their career for large amounts of money like this; perhaps they couldn't sell it for any amount of money. Over the years as they built up their repertoire and became more popular, their IP increased in value.

Obviously some IP will have little or no value in the marketplace whereas other IP may have tremendous value, and like tangible property the value depends on demand and supply and will differ at any given time. It's difficult to say whether our own IP will ever carry a price tag of $4 million, but why not use that amount as a milestone to which we can aspire! Surely you remember your high school teacher telling you if you try for an A, you'll get an A. If you aim just to pass the course by getting a D, that probably will be your grade. Content owners must be the first to believe that IP has real value in the real world, or that there is tangible value in intangible property. And hopefully, others too will believe it.

What Is the Value of Rights on the Net?

This is not the most accurate question to ask. The question at the heart of this discussion is what is the value of IP, period. Or, what is the value of IP on the Net as well as off the Net. The value of IP is not media specific. You build value through all of its uses in all media. Whether in digital or nondigital media, it has always been difficult to put a value on IP.

However, the digital media market is growing exponentially, and it is a market void of content, or at least useful, helpful content that people need. And it's likely that people will pay for the right kind of content — meaning that content creators will get paid for the right kind of content. This doesn't mean there is a fortune to be made in digital IP today; however, we can already see that it is an area with significant potential. In the infancy years of the digital era, much of the digitized content may be adapted from other forms, such as books and nondigitized music and videos, and the value of IP in nondigital forms will help put a dollar value on it in digital forms.

At the current time we do not know the value of most IP. What we do know is that certain IP has some value right now, and that in the future it will most likely have greater value. Its greater value will come from the confidence of content holders to demand more money for content and the public's willingness to pay for that content.

How Do I Begin?

If IP is so hard to place a value on, how does one begin to do so? Ask for as much as you can without laughing out loud! Or ask for the amount that makes you smile inside but allows you to keep an outward poker face. These are what I call "negotiating amounts" or "dream amounts." They are the actual amounts you might receive from a buyer of your IP — though they might not be. They are, however, the amounts which you can start with in order to value your IP. But keep in mind that despite the above rule of thumb, you want to price your IP at somewhat reasonable starting amounts. And from there, you can begin to discuss or negotiate what the interested buyer is willing and able to pay for it.

Promotional Value

IP owners negotiating for payment from the use of their IP on the Web often have to face Web site owners who don't want to pay in cash. Instead, they argue that the IP owners benefit from the promotion of their IP on the Web site, especially as endorsed by someone other than the IP owners themselves. In these situations, the Web site owner might offer the content owner a link to her own Web site or to her email address so that others who view her works can contact the content owner for potential paid uses of her IP. It is up to the IP owner in each individual circumstance to determine whether such promotion may be worth the lack of monetary payment. In some cases, it may make sense, while in others it may not. However, both IP owners and Web site owners have to realize that if creators were always only receiving the promotional benefit, then they would never earn any income from Internet uses.

Market Value

The value of IP is based on what the market will pay, which in turn is based on the value potential purchasers see in the property. However, when it comes to digital works, the market is so new that the value is not yet determined. There are as yet no such things as typical rates or industry standards for buying and selling digital property. And there are no concrete precedents as to whether photographers, illustrators, and animators should obtain a flat fee as payment or perhaps an advance with ongoing royalties from the sale of an end product incorporating their digital photograph or illustration. Much like cyberspace itself, this is an evolving topic, and as in any sales transaction, you will have to demonstrate the value or benefits of your property, your IP, to your potential customers. As digital media becomes more prevalent, industry standards and payment schemes will emerge which will provide a more consistent basis on which to negotiate the payment for digital property.

Factors to Consider When Valuing Digital Property

Below is a list of important questions to consider when valuing digital property, followed by a discussion of each point. You might want to add to this list as you become more experienced in licensing digital property, and you might also tailor it to your particular perspective as a buyer or seller of IP. But always keep in mind that valuing IP is done on an individual basis. You must always consider the particular circumstances in any given situation.

➡ What is the IP being licensed?

➡ When was the IP created?

➡ Has it previously been licensed in any forms or media? If so, at what value?

➡ Has the content owner sold other IP? If so, at what value?

➡ Is it one or a few works being licensed or a large body of works?

➡ Is the work being used in whole or in part?

➡ How will the work be used?

➡ How many copies of the IP will be made?

➡ How will the IP be delivered to the customer?

➡ What control will the IP owner have over the use of the IP?

➡ Will it be used by a developer or end-user?

➡ Will it be put to a commercial or noncommercial use?

➡ In what media will the content be used?

➡ In what countries will the content be used?

➡ For what length of time is the license?

➡ Is it likely that the content will be easily copied in the licensed use?

➡ Is the license exclusive or nonexclusive?

➡ What is the content owner's reputation in his/her/its own country and around the world?

➡ At what stage is the creator in his career, or the organization in its life?

➡ Is the creator likely to create much more work?

➡ What are others getting paid for similar IP?

➡ Are there nonmonetary benefits to consider?

➡ Who retains ownership in the IP?

➡ What are the terms and conditions attached to the license for the work?

What is the IP being licensed?

Different types of IP may have different value. For instance, a print article from a community newspaper may be worth less than a video clip from a popular television series like *Seinfeld*. A vacation photograph may have different value than a slide of a famous painting from an art gallery. Even the same IP may have different value in different circumstances. For instance, a previously published article may have different value than the same unpublished article; in some cases, the published article will have less value because it has already been seen by some people, whereas in other circumstances — if it were previously published in a prestigious magazine such as the *New Yorker*, for instance — it might have greater value than if unpublished.

When was the IP created?

IP "hot off the press" may have greater value than that from the day before. For instance, IP containing news would fall into this category. However, older IP that is hard to find, such as the back issues of a rare magazine, might attract greater value than the current issue of the magazine that is readily available. It is important to understand that IP may have a constantly changing value; some IP will increase in value over time (like a popular song), while other IP will decrease in value over time (possibly that containing dated news).

Has it previously been licensed in any forms or media? If so, at what value?

If your work is a photograph that was published in a print magazine and now a Web site owner is acquiring the rights to it, the fee paid for use in the print magazine may help establish the fee for the Web site use. It may be a similar fee or perhaps a percentage of the original fee.

Has the content owner sold other IP? If so, at what value?

If you've licensed other IP for use in the same or different media, what were you paid for that use? In other words, what values for your IP have already been established? In Hollywood, it is a common expression that you are only worth what you were paid for your last film (for actors and writers). Of course, in Hollywood, this amount is used as the beginning figure for negotiations. Why not try the same thing?

Is it one or a few works being licensed or a large body of works?

As in any sales transaction, the greater the quantity being purchased the better the price the owner might be willing to give. If one illustration is available for $100, you may choose to sell two illustrations for $180, or three for $250. Some food for thought.

Is the work being used in whole or in part?

A creator may charge less for the use of a part of a work. However, if the creator is concerned about the distortion of the work, he may charge more, or ask for safeguards against distortion of that use.

How will the work be used?

Will the work be used on a Web site or on an intranet? Will it be used in a CD-ROM? What about its use in an electronic database? Even if the value of your IP does not seem high, if you can license the same IP for different uses, then you will exponentially earn more income from the use of your IP. Always ask the licensee what he will be doing with the rights being licensed so that you can base your compensation on those uses. Also, if a licensee does not have plans to use a work, why license it to him?

There are many uses that are not yet thought of and which we cannot predict. If you do decide to license for future yet-to-be-discovered uses, make sure that your IP is adequately valued to cover any unanticipated profits to the licensee.

How many copies of the IP will be made?

Will the IP be used one time only in a slide presentation at a conference or will it be reproduced in ten thousand flyers? The more copies being made, the more you can expect for payment.

How will the IP be delivered to the customer?

IP that can be delivered to the customer online within seconds of the customer's request may have more value to the customer than IP that is delivered the next day or the next week.

What control will the IP owner have over the use of the IP?

If the IP owner loses all control over his work once it goes into the hands of the customer, then he may want to charge a higher fee for that IP. That is because he may lose other opportunities to sell that same IP if he cannot control it once it is licensed.

Will it be used by a developer or end-user?

A CD-ROM developer may pay more for the use of your photograph in her CD-ROM than a person posting your photo on their family Web site. On the other hand, the developer may be purchasing thousands of photographs for inclusion in the CD-ROM and may pay less than a corporation who licenses the same photograph for use on the cover of its annual report.

Will it be put to a commercial or noncommercial use?

Different uses require consideration when valuing IP. A for-profit corporation may pay more than a nonprofit organization or a small business person. An individual, library, school, or museum may not pay as much as a large corporation. However, a noncommercial use of your IP may entice you for different non-monetary reasons such as educating the public and exposure of your IP.

In what media will the content be used?

If you're licensing for use in a print book or magazine, you may charge a different fee than if the work is being used on a Web site to which the entire world may have access and possibly for free.

In what countries will the content be used?

In nondigital licensing arrangements, creators can often negotiate additional payments for each territory. For instance, if a creator sells U.S. rights, he is paid a certain fee; however, if he also sells Canadian and U.K. rights, the creator is paid further compensation. Generally, licensing for the Internet means global rights as opposed to licensing for use in a print book or CD-ROM where the territories of use can be more easily defined.

For what length of time is the license?

The general rule here is that the shorter the length of the license, the lower the fees paid to the creator.

Is it likely that the content will be easily copied in the licensed use?

If your IP can easily be copied, it may lose its value over time. For instance, if you license the use of a music clip for someone to post on their Web site and anyone can then copy that music, will you later be able to relicense that music or will the market then be unwilling to pay for it (if they can download it for free)? If it can be easily copied, you may want to ask for a higher fee; on the other hand, you may choose not to license it at all for that use, or may only license it once the music is placed in a "secure" section of the Web site where only people with a password can access it. Note that secure areas like this are only beginning to become popular. Also, you may ask the licensee if he is using encryption or watermarking, for instance, to ensure that the IP is not easily copied.

Is the license exclusive or nonexclusive?

Generally, higher compensation is paid for exclusive uses of IP since it means that you will not have the opportunity to sell the same IP at the same time for the same use. For instance, if you grant an exclusive license to a print book publisher to publish your book, then you cannot simultaneously enter into the same agreement with another print book publisher during the duration of your first agreement. However, if you license an article for nonexclusive use on one Web site, you may be able to license it for use on another Web site or to a corporation for use in their newsletter or intranet.

What is the content owner's reputation in his/her/its own country and around the world?

As with the Rolling Stones example above, an established creator will earn greater income from her IP because of her own reputation. Sometimes a licensee will pay a higher fee for uses in the creator's own country where her reputation is more widespread.

At what stage is the creator in his career, or the organization in its life?

Young creators usually cannot demand as much payment for their work as more established creators. Licenses for Web site use by young creators may help provide them with broader exposure, which can in turn enhance their reputation and increase the future value of their IP.

Is the creator likely to create much more work?

If so, this may make the work more valuable because the licensee can return again and again to the same creator to license more of her tried and tested property.

What are others getting paid for similar IP?

This is discussed in further detail below.

Are there nonmonetary benefits to consider?

If your IP is used on an educational Web site, it might be accessed by thousands of students and teachers who will then remember your name and buy your IP in other forms. If your work is used in association with a well-known museum, this may enhance your reputation. In these and other circumstances, it doesn't mean you should not get paid for IP, but that you should value your work at a price that takes into account all of the circumstances.

Who retains ownership in the IP?

If you assign the work and relinquish ownership, make sure you are adequately compensated as you will have no further rights in the work. On the other hand, if you provide a license to use the work and you retain ownership in it, you can price it lower as there may be additional markets in which you can license it.

Lastly, what are the terms and conditions attached to the license for the work?

The value of your IP cannot be established in isolation. Its value depends on the terms and conditions of the permissible uses of your IP — the topic of chapter 5.

What Others Are Paid

Knowing what others are paid for their IP can help you value your own IP. Generally, those who make a lot and those who make very little from their IP publicly share what they are paid for it. However, for the greater majority of people or organizations who sell or buy IP, there is no public registry, news reporting, or Web site dealing with the amount paid for that IP. Nonetheless, below are some of my findings.

A woman who was helping a dictionary expand its previous edition by about 20,000 words and who was asked to write definitions of new and existing words, provide examples of use of those words, etymologies, and phonetic transcriptions was being paid Can$2.50 per definition (her payment was cut later to $2.14 per definition).[3] You try placing a value on the definition of a single word!

In 1994, Bill Gates paid US$31.8 million to purchase a Leonardo da Vinci notebook in order to digitize it and include it in a CD-ROM.

The Cat in the Hat, et al.

Known as Dr. Seuss, Theodor Seuss Geisel, author and illustrator of forty-four books, and author of an additional fourteen books, which were translated into twenty languages, made a lot of money for himself as well as his publisher, Random House. During his lifetime, Dr. Seuss earned royalties from his print books in the amount of US$500 million. Although no "public" figures are available, the privately held Dr. Seuss Enterprises has supposedly earned US$7 million to $10 million a year in residuals, mostly from print books and television specials. Not bad for a man who supposedly said, after refusing a lucrative merchandising offer, that he would rather go into the *Guinness Book of Records* as the writer who refused the most money per word.

Celine

Let's look at a superstar like Celine Dion. With her fame, she can obtain a 25-percent royalty or more on the sale of every one of her CDs or cassettes. However, "nonstars" don't fare nearly as well and typically can obtain only a 14-percent royalty rate, of which 2 percent is the producer's royalty. The net rate of 12 percent is based on the retail price of the CD or cassette.

Sunset Boulevard

The budget figures for the Los Angeles run of the musical *Sunset Boulevard* shed some light on the value of IP. For the week of July 2, 1995, it cost US$731,304 to stage the show. Out of that amount, $41,929 was the composer's royalty, $16,771 was the producer's royalty, and $138,352 was spent on advertising fees. Interestingly, the show ultimately failed in terms of making money for its owners as the revenues didn't cover the costs. However, Andrew Lloyd Webber, who owns some of the copyrights to the tunes in the show, earns a fair return on his effort. He receives royalties on records and sheet music in addition to the shows, even when the shows are not making money. Further, as a producer entitled to royalties, his company can also make money even when the show loses. See the significance of owning IP!

Rent

The New York production of *Rent* will take in about US$26 million per year if it continues to sell out. In addition, money from road productions, cast albums, and film rights could ultimately generate hundreds of millions in total revenues.

And Then There's Jerry Garcia

As of February 1, 1997, the regular sources of estate income of Jerry Garcia, leader of the famed band the Grateful Dead, are royalties of approximately US$200,000 per year from Ben & Jerry's ice cream "conglomerate" for the use of the name "Cherry Garcia" as an ice cream flavor; approximately $300,000 per year in royalties from the Art Peddler for a tie-manufacturing contract and the sale of lithographs; and music publishing royalties of about $250,000 per year. Supposedly, more than 90 percent of the income earned by Jerry Garcia during his lifetime was from live concerts of the Grateful Dead.

Writers

Text in the form of articles, books, short stories, poems, and other works are much sought after content on the Internet. In fact, text is what most of us currently use from the Net, usually for free at this point in time. Since most print newspaper and magazine publishers sell entire newspapers or magazines, it is difficult for them to value an individual article or story. In some situations, writers are earning a percentage of their original fee for electronic uses, while others are obtaining flat fees. For instance, the Norwegian newspaper journalists association came to an agreement with newspapers in which it is acknowledged that the online transmission of stories or pictures constitutes a second publication, and consequently the writers are paid the equivalent of US$150 a year for their material when used on the Internet and US$75 for use in databases available to the public. In a Canadian example, one publisher is offering a flat fee of Can$100 for the first use of print book content on the Net or a commercial online service. One Canadian print newspaper publisher has paid some writers 100 percent of their print fee when republishing a story on its own newspaper CD-ROM.

Photographers

The fee that Corbis pays for a digitized image depends on whether it is a stock image or one prepared on an assignment basis. As of February 1996, for stock images, Corbis pays a US$4.50 per image advance against royalties in exchange for nonexclusive digital rights for a period of twenty years. When Corbis and its affiliates use these photographs in products produced by themselves, photographers have the choice of a variety of royalty options from 1 to 7 percent of sales depending on the circumstances. When stock sales are made to third parties, photographers receive 45 percent of sales. Photographers also have limited rights to reclaim certain images from Corbis if another of the photographer's clients wants to license exclusive rights in these images.

For assignments, Corbis pays photographers day rates from US$350 to $500, plus expenses. In addition, photographers receive a medical insurance subsidy and disability insurance during the term of the assignment. In this situation, Corbis retains the copyright to its selections, while photographers retain rights in "rejected" images. Supposedly, 60 to 80 percent of the images are returned to the photographer. Photographers also receive 10 percent of any sales of the selected images for a period of ten years. Lastly, photographers may use the selected images in personal promotions and monographs (such as print books.)[4]

Museums and Art Galleries

As with individuals, institutions do not yet have set fee schedules or common practices for licensing images in their collections. Many institutions license images as a way to earn revenue as well to meet the goals of their educational mandate.

One U.S. art gallery with whom I discussed "value" decides each licensing request on a case-by-case basis and takes into account the many surrounding factors, such as intended use of the image (in a video game versus an encyclopedia, for instance). As an example, this institution has charged a college professor US$10 for use of an image in its collection and a corporation in the range of US$100 to $2,000 per image, and sometimes even more. The gallery always insists on an acknowledgment of the source of the image, thereby raising its own profile with the hope of encouraging the public to come and see the original works. Interestingly, this gallery digitizes all images itself and it watermarks all of these digitized images.

One Canadian museum charges between Can$50 and $200 for the use of a single digitized image from its collection. However, it did charge $10 per image as a "volume discount" in one situation where it licensed twenty-one images for use in a CD-ROM.

Value in a Worldwide Market

In determining a value for IP, you have to consider the size of your market. Any digital property sold on the Net automatically has a worldwide market. With such a huge marketplace, it is possible to sell your IP for a few cents, or less, and still make a significant amount of money from it. So the consumer and you both win.

However, because of the nature of the Internet with its roots in providing free information to the public, many users have reservations against paying for packaged information. And in some situations, consumers believe that any cost for content on the Internet would be expensive. In fact, the reverse may be true. With a worldwide market, content owners may be in a position where they can charge very little per use, as it is the cumulative collection of payment that provides them with their "due" compensation.

There are microcommerce systems on the Internet that support this thinking. Millicent (*http://www.research.digital.com/SCR*

/*millicent*/) is one such system designed to help content owners sell their content over the Web for fractions of a cent. These microcommerce systems support Web transactions as small as one-tenth of a cent and attempt to attract content owners selling articles, cartoons by the strip, and individual songs. The Millicent Project supports small pay-per-use fees such as simple, one-page national weekly magazine articles at two cents, longer feature articles at twenty-five cents, and political cartoons at less than one cent. This system can sell all content including text, audio broadcasts, songs, video clips, computer software, and documentation. (See chapter 3 for a discussion of Millicent and other microcommerce systems.)

Is There a Service Involved?

In some IP arrangements, you sell your IP by itself as an individual product. In others, there are related services, updates to the original work, or ancillary products which you might be involved in selling and providing. When valuing your IP, you must have to look at the overall picture. For instance, is the e-zine the main product and primary source of revenue or is it an advertisement/promotion to sell your other services and perhaps further IP or ancillary products? Are you providing free updates to your IP on a Web site? If it's the main product, you might want to price it higher than if it's more of an advertisement or a way to attract further revenue.

A Tip

Because digital rights are new, many people think that they have or will have tremendous value. However, at the current time, there may not be much money deriving from the exploitation of digital property. In some situations, people are declining to license their own digital property because they believe they are being offered an inadequate amount for their rights. As a suggestion, if someone is not able or willing to pay what you believe is the value of your digital rights, do not walk away. There may be alternative arrangements for you to consider and negotiate with a potential purchaser of your IP. If the lump sum you're offered is too low, ask for a percentage of profits. If you're still unhappy, limit the duration of the license, or make sure it is nonexclusive, and for one or two digital rights and not all of them. Another suggestion is to ask for a nominal amount as payment for your IP. For instance, ask for $10. Then next time, ask for $15. And the time after that, ask for $20. Hopefully, over time, you'll be able to establish a "fair market" value for your IP.

E-Rights as Secondary Rights

In some situations, especially during the growth of new media, many works being licensed are ones that have previously been licensed. For instance, an article or cartoon strip that appeared in a print newspaper might be posted on that or another newspaper's Web site. In some of these cases, a creator may obtain as payment a percentage of the original (or print) fees. For example, a newspaper might offer a writer 30 percent of the original fee for its Web site use. In other cases, the writer might be offered a flat fee. Creators will have to negotiate the amount they see as fair payment in these situations. Creators may be able to license these secondary rights again and again, and what might seem to be smaller fees for a second or third use, if sold many times, can be a larger amount.

Negotiating, Agents, and Lawyers

> *This contract is so one-sided that I am surprised to find it written on both sides of the paper.*
> — Lord Evershed

As in most business transactions, negotiation skills can determine the dollar amount you receive for your digital property, as well as the related terms and conditions of its use. Understanding the industry in which you are working and the nature of the individual or organization with whom you are dealing will put you in a better negotiating position. Understanding the negotiating process will also help you.

Many content creators are not comfortable negotiating arrangements and would rather not represent themselves in such situations. Lawyers can represent you (though often at their hourly rate), and "agents" can also do so (usually for a 10 to 15 percent cut of your moneys earned from the arrangement). The role of lawyers is further discussed in chapter 9.

Agents as we traditionally know them in the publishing and film businesses are just starting to get their feet wet in representing digital content creators. However, agents can play a more extensive role than just negotiating deals on your behalf. For instance, an agent may help manage your career, suggest possible profitable projects, help find collaborators, and alert a new media producer to your talent and work. Agents may also guide you to selling your IP in various media, including print, radio, television, film, and digital uses. And they may help you gain exposure as a creator, which in turn may help increase the value of your IP. The role of your agent is a matter between you and your agent — a matter you should discuss, and probably put in writing, prior to having that agent represent you.

Competing with Free IP

I have heard it said that it is ignoble for authors, who seek fame as the reward of their writings, to ask for payment too. This is well said; fame is attractive. But it must be remembered that, to enjoy it for only a single year, nature condemns one to eat at least 365 times.

— Beaumarchais (1732–1799)

Notwithstanding everything said thus far, some IP is intentionally given away for free. Sure, we all might write an article for a local newspaper and not receive any payment, but what we're talking about here goes much beyond that. We're talking about large companies, as well as starting companies or individuals, giving away their IP as a way for that property to attain its value. Computer software is one of the biggest examples of this. Microsoft, for example, gives a lot of its software away for free: Microsoft Internet Explorer has been free since it was introduced in 1995. This free distribution built it a large customer base — and also caused its competitors to be creative in order to stay in the market.

This is important vis-à-vis the new media entrepreneur who produces his own products and distributes them. How is he to price his product? And can he afford to give it away for free? Rest assured, most of us cannot afford to give it away for free. But that's where we are seeing an interesting move on the Internet and where some compare it to other media models like broadcasting or those free magazines thrown on your doorstep. In these other media, what is free to the public is paid for by advertisers. So what seems free to you and me is costing someone else big bucks and often also benefitting someone (the broadcaster or publisher in these examples) with those big bucks.

Further, many Web site owners are providing content for free in order to sell other products and services. For example, the Web site for my book *Canadian Copyright Law* (*http://www.mcgrawhill.ca/copyrightlaw/*) provides free content on various copyright issues for creators and users of copyright materials, as well as for specific interest groups like librarians and archivists, corporations, and Internet users. One chapter of the book is posted on the site. There is a FAQ (frequently asked questions) section on the site where people are encouraged to email the book's author (me!) with their questions, and we periodically post the answers to the most common ones. All this information is provided for free, with the hope of us selling more books. And I also get email from potential clients for my law practice.

Another concept to keep in mind is that people often do not value content on the Web because it's free, and we seem to have this perception that if you pay for it, then it is better, more valuable information.

Museums, Libraries, Galleries, and Archives

Most of this chapter has been directed towards the individual content creator. However, there are many institutional IP owners, including organizations like MGM, Disney Studios, the Smithsonian, the National Archives of Canada, and the Louvre. Some of these organizations have had much experience buying and selling IP and therefore valuing their IP. For example, Hollywood film studios understand the value of their film libraries. Museums, libraries, and others have had much less experience putting a value on their collections or IP, but they are quickly beginning to realize that there is a value, evidenced by Corbis buying up the e-rights to museum collections around the world. The question here is, how do these institutions value their IP?

The elements set out in this chapter which give IP its value can equally be applied by a museum or library when determining at what price to sell its IP. As in other situations, the value of digitized collections and any IP is very much what the market will pay.

Public institutions are faced with a further issue in valuing their IP. There is often a clash between their role as a cultural and educational institution and their need to operate as a viable business. In the digital world, some people even hold certain institutions responsible for preserving our "digital heritage." As a result, the value of licensing their digital property has to be examined in terms of both monetary and nonmonetary benefits to the institution.

Final Word

There are no hard and fast rules for determining the value of your IP. All of the relevant circumstances must be taken into account, from the reputation of the creator to the intended use of the work to the number of copies being made. It is usually a matter of negotiation and of what the market/consumer will pay for the IP. And with the newness of new media and the Internet, it is likely that the value of IP next year will be higher than this year, and even higher the following year. Once you determine the value of your IP, you will need to enter into the proper licensing arrangements, the topic of the next chapter.

End Notes

1. Stacy Snowman, "Conducting Intellectual Property Audits 1996," 429 PLI/Pat 7 at 9.

2. Kevin Goldman, "A Few Rockers Give Ad Makers No Satisfaction," *Wall Street Journal*, 25 August 1995, p. B1.

3. Rebecca Carpenter, "Defining Moments," *Saturday Night*, March 1997, p. 69.

4. David Walker, "The World According to Corbis," *PDN Photo District News* 16, no. 2 (February 1996).

PART 3
Making Money

CHAPTER 5

Selling and Licensing Digital Property

A verbal contract isn't worth the paper it's written on.

— Samuel Goldwyn, Hollywood movie producer

Now that we've dealt with the money aspect, we must turn our attention to "rights" issues. As you know, the value of IP is closely connected to the rights you're licensing. Let's look at an example of how this works. Take a photograph. You could sell all the rights in your photograph to company A for $100. Alternatively, you could sell the rights to include your photograph in a print book about geography to company B for $75, the right to include it on company C's Web site for $60, and the right for it to appear on postcards to company D for $50. As you can see, there is value to selling *all* rights in your photograph to company A, but this simplified example also shows that an outright sale of rights may result in less money being paid to you than the accumulated payments from licensing the same photograph to companies B, C, and D. This case illustrates an important point: the terms and conditions surrounding the licensing of your digital property help determine its value. This chapter examines some of these terms and conditions.

Licensing Arrangements

A licensing arrangement contains the particular circumstances that an IP owner and a user/"purchaser" agree upon for the use of certain specified IP. The details agreed upon are usually set out in a written form called a *license agreement* or *contract*. In simpler terms, a license agreement or contract means *permission* to use certain IP.

As a content owner, you require a license agreement whenever someone else uses your content. As a user of content, you need a license agreement whenever you use the content of others.

There are a myriad of possible licensing arrangements. In fact, any arrangement is possible (read: time for creativity) as long as the parties involved agree to it. As a creator/owner of content or as someone acquiring it, you may be involved in some of these possible scenarios:

→ licensing a handful of works to be used in association with works by other creators (for instance, licensing three photographs for use on a Web site with other photographs, text, animation, etc.)

→ licensing all of the works to appear in a new media product (for example, a museum might license digital rights to its Picasso collection for use by a developer in a CD-ROM strictly about Picasso works in that museum)

→ licensing works for "relicensing" purposes (you might license the rights to digitize your articles or images to one company which will then relicense these rights to CD-ROM producers, Web site owners, corporations, and others)

Other scenarios might involve being commissioned to create new works for inclusion in a new media product. Or you might be on the other side, hiring someone as an employee or as a freelancer to create some or all of the IP to be included in your new media product. Often a new media product is a combination of the above arrangements, and the license agreement will reflect the various related terms concerning the use of IP.

Some new media developers use public domain works, whose copyright protection has expired, so that they do not need to clear any rights. Further, with new media products, many creators publish their own works, which is a very viable option. You may publish your art in your own online gallery, or your articles in your own e-zine. Of course, you probably won't need a license agreement if you decide to publish your own works. Throughout any negotiation process for licensing your rights to someone else, keep in mind that, if you are unhappy with what you are negotiating, you may prefer to be your own publisher and become a new media entrepreneur.

The Nature of Transferring Rights

Before examining specific terms and conditions in a license agreement, you should have a full understanding of the term *licensing*. In simple terms, *licenses* and *assignments* are two ways to allow others to use your IP. An assignment is like a sale or transfer of rights — when you "assign" your rights, you are permanently giving away your IP, or a part thereof. A license is comparable to a lease or a rental of rights — when you "license" a piece of your IP, you are temporarily permitting someone else to use it.

Using the word *assignment* or *license* may not by itself guarantee the type of rights grant you wish to make. The wording used in a license agreement could be such that, in practice, it has a similar effect to an assignment. The key concept to understand is that your rights may be exploited (usually in exchange for money) without necessarily being sold or permanently given away to someone else.

Note that this book sometimes uses the term *purchaser* of IP to refer both to assignment and licensing situations although there is no actual change of ownership in a license situation. This is because the "purchaser" purchases the right to use a work in a certain manner even though he may not acquire outright ownership of that right or work. Similarly, this book uses the terms *buying* and *selling* IP, which in most circumstances refer to licensing IP. These are terms and meanings used in the marketplace and something you should be aware of.

Controlling Your Works (Nonexclusive Licenses)

License agreements allow owners to maintain greater control over their works (in terms of resale rights and adaptations, for instance) and are popular in the computer software industry.

One important advantage of a license over an assignment, especially with respect to new media, is that the same right or work can be licensed to more than one person or organization at a time. This is called a nonexclusive license. For example, a nonexclusive license may be given to many movie theaters to show a particular film. A "licensee" (as defined below) should know when he is obtaining a nonexclusive license and be aware of the fact that others may be able to make the same and/or a different use of the work.

Many people or organizations who license IP (called "licensees") require an exclusive license. A print book publisher, for instance, needs that commitment of exclusivity before expending effort and expense in publishing a book. However, the same is not true, and in many instances is the reverse, when it comes to new media. Because of the ever changing nature of new media products and the fact that many works in a new media product are very small components (for example, one of a thousand works in a CD-ROM) as opposed to the *only* work (a manuscript for a print book), nonexclusive licenses are popular. For licensees, this often means paying less for the right or work. And for content owners, it often means selling for less, but with the possibility of sales for the many other licenses adding up to more than what they could obtain from a single, exclusive license. Therefore, it's a win-win situation.[1]

Terms and Conditions

> *You should have let me in on this. We could have*
> *planned it, prepared it, presold the movie rights!*
> — Jim Carrey, in *Batman Forever* (written by Lee Batchler and
> Janet Scott Batchler)

New media law, similar to the technology itself, is constantly changing, as is the nature of legal arrangements and the ways to license IP for use in new media products. As such, any discussion of relevant terms and conditions should be carefully reviewed in light of the most up-to-date technological and legal developments, and in light of your own circumstances. For instance, a museum may have different concerns and issues to address in a license agreement for the use of works in its collection than would a photographer or journalist. Nonetheless, below are some important clauses for all content owners and users to consider when negotiating and drafting an agreement. Depending on your circumstances, you will need to adapt these clauses, or ignore them, or include other clauses in your own license agreements. Hopefully, the clauses below will provide you and your lawyers with some guidelines in this area. As stated elsewhere in this book, this discussion is for informational purposes only, and I encourage you to seek proper legal counsel before entering into any license agreements.

As a generic discussion on this topic, these licensing clauses are intended for licensors and licensees, and for individuals, corporations, museums, archives, libraries, and any others involved in the licensing of IP.

License: Permission to use a copyright work without any transfer of ownership in that work.

License agreement: A document, usually written, that sets out the terms and conditions under which a licensor grants permission to a licensee to use his intellectual property.

Licensor: The party in a license agreement who owns the intellectual property being licensed.

Licensee: The party in a license agreement who is being granted permission to use intellectual property.

Clauses in License Agreements

Preamble

Typically, license agreements begin with a preamble stating the legal names and addresses of the owner of the content (licensor) and the person/organization acquiring or "licensing" the use of that content (licensee). These would be the two or more parties to the agreement. If the licensor has acquired some of the rights from a third party, this is also typically reflected in the preamble.

Definitions

The agreement sets out and defines certain terms used in it, especially where such terms can have more than one meaning. Commonly defined terms include *product, commercial use, noncommercial use, digitize, image, platform, work, territory*, and *content*.

The agreement should define the subject matter being addressed. The subject matter can be defined in terms of specific works, such as *Kyle's Book on Bicycles*, published by ABC Publisher in 1995, which is to be digitized, or it can be more generally defined — for instance, the text and images and audiovisual works owned by (or in the collection of) XYZ Museum as of January 1, 1997. All works that are the subject of the agreement, such as text, images, databases, laptop-based and multimedia presentations, musical works, sound recordings, videos, and computer software, should be mentioned. If the list is very long and/or is subject to changes or additions, you might add it as an appendix to the license agreement.

Rights Granted/License

> *Under no circumstances should a writer sign for more than a single [radio] performance of his script.*
>
> — Norman Corwin, *Authors Guild Bulletin* (1944)

This clause is the essence of the agreement. It sets out the rights the licensor is granting to the licensee. Sometimes this portion of the agreement is divided into two parts: rights granted to the licensee, and rights not granted to the licensee. In addition, the agreement might state that all rights not specifically granted to the licensee remain with the licensor. This is important as you want to be clear about who owns the rights.

This is a good place in your agreement to mention whether the license is exclusive or nonexclusive. IP owners should be aware that when you enter into an exclusive license or assignment arrangement, you are also excluding *yourself* from using the work in the manners set out in the arrangement.

The scope of this rights clause is very important. The definition of rights can be as narrow or as broad as the parties agree. The broadest transfer would transfer the entire copyright, while a narrow permission may be the inclusion of a specific portion of a photograph on a Web site for a thirty-day period.

Unless the entire copyright is assigned, you will need to spell out the various rights being licensed. There are no special rules or words for spelling out these rights. However, whatever wording is employed, ensure that it is clear and covers the applicable uses of the works being licensed. For instance, if a work is being published online, applicable rights might include reproduction, adaptation, transmission, broadcasting, communication to the public, performance in public, public display, and public exhibition, depending on the wording used in the laws of any one country. However, because the Internet is borderless, it may be a good idea to cover all possibilities by including rights that exist not only in your own country but in other countries where the works may be used.

Some of the many important rights include the right to digitize, synthesize, produce, reproduce, publish, republish, modify, enhance, adapt, value-add, translate, use in association with other works, advertise, publicly display, exhibit, distribute, transmit, broadcast, publicly perform, publicly communicate, license, sub-license (see below), sell, rent, catalog, back up, archive, include in a database, index, and to authorize any of these rights.

Prior to buying or selling IP, consider to what use(s) the work(s) will be put, and have your agreement reflect these uses in the rights granted clause. Although some purchasers would like agreements for the use of works in any medium, whether now in existence or in existence in the future, this tends to scare off content owners who may be cautious in licensing possible uses of their works in relation to yet-to-be discovered technologies. We have already seen this in relation to pre-Internet agreements. For example, a copyright holder who transferred all rights in her work three years ago under an agreement with a broad clause, and without ever knowing about the Web, may now find her work on the Web without further compensation for that Web site use. Further, it may mean that licensees are paying for rights which they do not use. Where content buyers want to address rights for future technology in their license agreements, one approach might be to include a clause that states that the parties will later negotiate fair and reasonable terms for such unpredictable uses at the time on a case-by-case basis. (This is further addressed below under the clause "Rights in Future Works.")

E-Rights

The concept of electronic rights, called e-rights, and also referred to as digital rights, is not specifically defined in the copyright statutes of most countries. However, e-rights may include rights for use in CD-ROMs, DVDs, online, Internet, intranets, extranets, Web sites, databases, and archives. As the technology changes, so will the meaning of electronic rights, and possibly the meaning of "platforms" like CD-ROMs and DVDs. This is why it is very important for agreements to refer to specific uses and rights as opposed to general, broad concepts like "electronic rights" and "digital media" and "online use." Even the Internet may be replaced by some other means of digital distribution and storage in the next several years, and an agreement limiting use to the Internet could in fact unintentionally limit future uses by a licensee. On the other hand, an IP owner may deliberately want to limit certain unknown future uses.

Licensees who develop new media products should be careful to ensure that they secure any necessary rights beyond the e-rights. For instance, a DVD developer may want to advertise the product through print media (newspapers, flyers, postcards, etc.), and without some "print" rights, the developer may not be able to show the content of the DVD as an example or demo of how wonderful the product is.

Media Limitations

Many things are about to happen before others begin.
— Stephen Leacock, *The Yahi-Bahi Oriental Society*

In addition to the rights being licensed, an agreement may restrict use of the content to specific media. For instance, if you have the right to use content for a television program, you do not necessarily have the right to use that content on the Internet. As discussed above, as a licensee, you must be careful to license all the necessary rights for current and possibly future media (for example, you do not want the problem of owning film rights but not having video rental rights). In the same vein, as a content owner, you may want to limit the media, or at least ensure that for each different medium you are entitled to further payment.

Some relevant media include CD-ROMs, Internet, intranets, extranets, databases, archives, and Web sites. Also, keep in mind that the Internet and other media might change in the future but keep the same name. Thus, any possible detailed descriptions to define the Internet or other terms might help clarify the uses permitted by the license agreement.

As a practical matter, an agreement could set out a payment attached to each use (CD-ROM use, Internet use, database use, etc.). This way, it is clear to both owner and buyer that each use is separate and that each use has a separate compensation associated with it. This may also help ensure that the content owner is compensated for newer generations of digital technology.

Usage

Usage, especially when licensing e-rights, is an important consideration. For example, terms and conditions as well as pricing may vary depending on whether your IP is used for foreground or background purposes. For example, is your photograph the opening image on a Web site or used on a subsequent Web page as background for text?

Moral Rights

Only the author or actual creator of a copyright-protected work can possess the moral rights in it. In other words, moral rights cannot be transferred like other rights in copyright. However, you may still need to address the issue of whether the creator retains moral rights in the works being licensed. These include the right to have the creator's name on the work and to prevent damaging modifications to the work that may be prejudicial to the reputation of the creator.

Some countries, including the United States, have more limited moral rights protection, and if a content owner is licensing with a U.S. company or individual, this may be a point to specifically raise. Moral rights provisions are more popular in countries like the United Kingdom and Canada. Note, however, that in these countries, their laws allow for a waiver of moral rights, which means that the creator can agree not to exercise her rights, and often this is set out in the agreement. This is a point of negotiation. If the work is one out of a thousand works on a Web site, it may be reasonable for the creator to waive her moral rights. On the other hand, if that creator's work is a "major" component of the Web site, it might make sense in the circumstances that the author's name appear in association with her work. Some countries like France do not allow for a waiver of moral rights, and therefore any licensee must respect the moral rights of creators.

Where the license is granted by a creator, as opposed to an owner who did not actually create the IP, the licensee may be able to obtain a waiver of moral rights from that creator (in countries where this is permissible). However, if the party to the agreement is the owner and not the actual creator of the IP, the licensee may require some sort of warranty from the IP owner that he obtained a waiver of moral rights (where permissible) from which the licensee can also benefit.

Underlying Rights

Because of the different layers of protection in IP, licensors must ensure that they own the rights they purport to license, and licensees will want to address this issue. In fact, a prudent licensee might ask for proof from the licensor of written release forms from the owners of underlying rights. To illustrate this underlying rights issue, a licensor may own the right in an audiovisual work, but not the right in the script underlying it, and the licensee may require both rights in order to proceed with her own new media product.

Further, a licensor may need copyright permissions and moral rights waivers (where permissible) for works or parts of works created by employees and freelancers/consultants. Similarly, a licensee may require written proof of such permissions and waivers.

Other Rights

Certain other non-IP legal issues may be addressed in the license agreement, including performers' rights, union reuse rights and residual payments, publicity and privacy rights, libel and slander, patents, trademarks, and confidential information. In general, the licensee will want a guarantee from the licensor that none of these additional rights are being infringed and that, where necessary, payments have been made, and permissions and releases obtained. Some of these additional rights are discussed in further detail in chapter 9.

Territory

A content owner may license a right either generally or subject to territorial limitations. This means that an author may grant a right "worldwide" (for use in the entire world), or within certain territories, such as North America, the United States, or the United Kingdom. Generally, the size of the territory is irrelevant, and there are no restrictions on the segmentation of geographical location to which a copyright can be assigned. In practice, however, it is unusual to divide copyright among a jurisdiction smaller than a country, although "English language throughout Canada" or "French language throughout Canada" is a commonly seen exception to this practice.

If a work is being posted on the Internet, the concept of a geographical boundary may not exist. At the current time, the Internet is by its nature global and encompasses the entire world. However, since we cannot predict whether the Internet will always be global (as much as this seems likely right now), it is best to refer to worldwide rights even with respect to the Internet. If the use of the work is for a new media product like a CD-ROM, then the license of rights could be for specific territories such as the United Kingdom or North America, or English-speaking countries. The larger the territory, the larger the payment, and the owner of the IP should ask for additional payment for worldwide use. In e-licensing, the trend is toward world or global licensing.

Where licensors are granting worldwide rights in IP, licensees may want some assurance from the licensors that they do in fact possess the applicable worldwide rights, as it is possible that the content owner assigned ownership or licensed some or all rights in the IP to others for use in one or more other countries or territories. Like many other provisions, this would appear in the warranties section of the license agreement.

Sublicenses

This clause would deal with whether and under what conditions the licensee may license the rights to others. For instance, if the licensor licenses Web site rights to the licensee, does the licensee have the right to authorize visitors to its Web site to use these licensed works? This is important as the end-user or Web site visitor is actually making a reproduction by visiting the site, or downloading it, or printing it and forwarding it to others.

In certain circumstances, a licensor may want to exclude multiple "hard copy" rights from a Web site or other new media license agreement, and to permit only a single paper copy per end-user or consumer of the Web site or other new media product, for personal, noncommercial use and not for resale. This would help to ensure that content owners are compensated for additional uses of their works by sublicensees.

Compensation (Money!)

Aren't we due a royalty statement?
— Charles, Prince of Wales, to his literary agent

Chapter 4 dealt with the value of your digital property. Related to the value of digital property is the structure of payment for the licensed use of your digital property. The compensation clause may specify a one-time flat fee (sometimes called a lump sum payment) for a specific use or uses, or it may stipulate ongoing payments based upon the quantity of products sold, or revenue (net or gross) earned therefrom, incorporating the licensed digital property. These latter arrangements are referred to as royalties. Part of these royalties may be paid up-front, called a royalty advance. The amount is negotiable.

A royalty advance is usually recoupable against future earnings. For instance, a writer may get a royalty advance upon signing a contract with a print book publisher. When the book is published and sold in the marketplace, the writer may be entitled to royalties based upon a percentage of the sale price of the book. Before paying the writer any royalties, the publisher will first deduct any royalty advances made to her. In that sense, the advance is recoupable. The manner in which royalties and advances are set out in an agreement varies according to the industry (film, book publishing, new media, visual arts, etc.). Specific industry associations may be able to guide you on these matters.

Alternatively, the "film model" may be followed with respect to licensing IP for use in new media products. Generally, in the television and film industry, there exists an "option" and an "option fee." An option gives the licensee the right to do certain things with your work, like use it to locate financing for the film. Upon certain occurrences, the option is exercised and the IP is "purchased" for an agreed upon option fee.

The new media industry is a hybrid between the publishing industry and the film industry, with some elements of uniqueness all its own. One unique model is that of earning money through the number of visitors to a Web site or the amount of time a consumer spends in a Web site. Payment can be based on these factors as well as the more traditional formulas such as royalties, lump sums, and options, or any combination of these. Whatever you negotiate, the agreement should clearly set out how payment is to be calculated, when it is to be received by the licensee, whether it is subject to any deductions, whether a payment statement will accompany it, and what currency it will be in. Related to this, the licensor may want a right to audit the accounts of the licensee to ensure that proper payment is being made.

Entertainment unions for writers, performers, and others are beginning to enter the new media realm. In general, these unions ensure that their members are paid minimum amounts of money for the use of their works under certain terms and conditions. As the new media industry grows, it is likely that the unions will play a greater role.

Copyright Ownership in Digital Works

> *As the [Canadian copyright] act now stands, it was pointed out, the right is given to exhibitions, fairs, churches and charitable organizations to perform musical compositions without the consent of the copyright owner and without remuneration to the author of the music or other copyrightable material. This, it was contended, was "unfair to intellectual labor."*
>
> — The Globe (1931)

The "ownership" clause is discussed here especially in relation to a work being licensed that is not initially in a digital format.

For instance, if an individual licenses a photograph, or a museum a slide of an item from its collection, or a print publisher a book, who owns the right in the digitized version of the photograph, slide, or book? Issues to be discussed and included in this clause are:

(a) which party is responsible for digitizing the nondigital work?

(b) who owns the rights in the underlying work?

(c) who owns the rights in the digital work?

(d) if the digitizer/new media developer owns the rights in the digital version, what can be done with that digitized version?

(e) can the owner of the underlying work make its own digital version or allow others to do so, and for what purposes?

Duration of Grant of Rights (Term of Agreement)

A license should state a definite beginning and end to the period of time in which rights may be exercised.

Rights can be licensed for different periods of time, such as for the duration of copyright protection or for shorter periods like six months or five years. Generally, the shorter the time, the less money it costs to license those rights. There is no minimum length of time for which a license may endure.

Different licenses may last for varying lengths of time. For instance, a license to A to include a work on its intranet may last for three years, while B may have the right to simultaneously include the same work on its Web site for eight years, after which time C may digitally archive the work for internal purposes for the next twenty-five years.

An agreement could include an automatic renewal upon certain conditions. For instance, the licensee may notify the licensor thirty days prior to the expiration of the agreement that the license will be extended for, let's say, three additional years, under the same terms and conditions as set out in the original agreement. Again, this is a matter of negotiation.

If the licensor has the right to terminate the agreement prior to the termination date set out in it, the circumstances in which this arises should be set out.

Revocation of Rights

Chances are, upon termination of the agreement at the specified number of years set out in it (provided it is not renewed), rights in the licensed property revert back to the licensor. However, the licensee may be able to continue to sell the new media products made during the life of the agreement. If so, the contract may state that the licensor is still entitled to payment (where applicable) for products sold after the termination of the agreement. This is traditionally limited in time (for instance, for six months from the termination of the agreement), and occasionally the licensor may even ask for all products incorporating the IP to be destroyed by a specific date set out in the agreement.

Further, if either party does not comply with the agreement, it may terminate prior to the termination date set out in the agreement. In contemplation of this, the agreement should address the rights and obligations of each party upon such early termination, including the reversion of rights in the licensed property to the licensor.

An important consideration in digital licensing is revocation in cases of non-use of certain rights. At the current time, some companies are licensing e-rights because it is a trend, yet they may in fact hold onto those rights without actually using them. Or the company might use the CD-ROM rights but not the Web site rights. It is suggested that in a five-year agreement, for example, if some of the rights are not exercised by a certain date, let's say the end of the second year, they revert to the licensor so that the licensor has an opportunity to license them to a different party and benefit therefrom, or exploit them herself.

Further, one should be aware of any statutory reversion of rights provisions whereby an assignment is only valid for a specified number of years. For instance, in Canada, certain assignments are limited to a maximum of twenty-five years, after which the rights revert to the author of the copyright work.[2]

Other situations where rights might revert back to the licensor are upon the insolvency, receivership, bankruptcy, or liquidation of the licensee, or where the product is no longer available to the public (usually for a fee), which is called "out of print" in the print book publishing industry.

Sequels, Editions, and Adaptations

Because new media products are often evolving or considered "live" products, it is important for your license agreements to discuss the use of IP in a subsequent version of the product. For instance, does your agreement provide for content licensed for use in one version of a CD-ROM to be used in the next edition of the CD-ROM, or in an upgrade, or how about in a foreign-localized version? Will the licensor provide the content for the updated version (and how will he be compensated for that)? If not, does the licensor have the right to approve changes and adaptations, as well as sequels and editions prepared by someone other than himself? And how will this affect the payment to the licensor from, and the credits (see below) that appear on, further versions?

Confidential Information

Often confidential information about the other party's business or products is shared between the licensor and licensee. License agreements often contain a provision to outline and define the nature of such confidential information, the fact that it is confidential and cannot be used by the other party or disclosed to any third parties, and that any items or works containing confidential information must be returned to the appropriate party upon the termination of the agreement.

Transferability

As new media companies may come and go quickly, it is important for a license agreement to address the issue of whether the agreement can be automatically transferred to a subsequent entity (i.e., a new owner of the company/licensee), or whether such a transfer requires the approval of the licensor. If the original agreement will be honored and the compensation paid, it may make sense for a licensor to permit the agreement to be transferred to a new company as it means that the IP owner does not have to start from scratch finding a licensee and negotiating an agreement. Approval of the transfer by the licensor allows him to examine the particular circumstances when they arise.

Credits

The licensor may want specific mention of his name in any new media product created by the licensee. If so, this should be set out in the license agreement. Specifics can include wording, size, and prominence of the credit. Where the licensed IP is to appear on the Internet, the licensor may request a link to her email address or the address (URL) of her own Web site. A licensor may want to ensure that any sublicensees are also subject to the credit obligations.

A licensee should be cautious about how the licensor's name will appear, especially in new media products where there can easily be hundreds or thousands of content owners, and should decide about the licensor's credit based on the circumstances in each license agreement and in relation to the new media product in which the licensed works will appear.

Delivery

Because of the intangible nature of IP, the form and method of its delivery to the licensee is important. Is it on a computer disk or online, in what computer program, etc.? The exact nature of delivery as well as the time and place should be set out in the agreement.

Complimentary Copies

In print book publishing, it is the norm for a writer to receive at least ten free copies of her book. Depending on the nature of the new media product, the issue of complimentary copies might be addressed. For instance, a licensor may be entitled to some free copies of a CD-ROM. However, it should be kept in mind that if there are hundreds of content owners involved, the licensee will not be able to afford to provide complimentary copies to each contributor. Also, with respect to online products, this sort of clause may have less relevance if the product (e.g., a Web site) is available to the public for free, or the clause may need to be adapted to reflect a situation where the IP is posted in a secure environment where only users with a password can access it.

Copyright Warnings

Print book publishing agreements often include the exact wording of the copyright notice to be set out in the published book. In e-publishing, you may also request that the exact wording of the notice be set out in the license agreement. In addition, you may request that the Web site owner or other new media developer include a copyright warning on the Web site or other new media product (e.g., CD-ROM). The warning may say something to the effect that the work is subject to copyright laws of a certain country and through the international system of copyright protection and that any uses beyond private, noncommercial, and nonprofit uses require the permission of the copyright owner.

Warranties

Licensees usually request that licensors warrant that they can enter into the license agreement. Licensors might warrant that they own or have cleared all the necessary rights in relation to any works subject to the agreement and that they have not infringed upon any rights relating to IP, privacy, or publicity, nor included any libelous or pornographic materials, or other illegal or unauthorized works. New media licensees may ask for this warranty on a worldwide basis.

Indemnity

Related to the warranties, the licensee may ask the licensor to indemnify him from any legal expenses and related claims arising from the warranties in the agreement. Although this provides some "security" to licensees, licensees should be cautious in relying upon them — they are only as good as the solvency of the licensor, and rights disputes can be costly.

Boilerplates

There are a number of "generic" clauses in any sort of agreement, usually set out at the end of the agreement. Some of these clauses are listed below.

➡ **Choice of law** — states that the laws of a specified state/ province and country apply to the agreement

➡ **Arbitration** — provides a fast (and less expensive than legal proceedings) way to resolve any dispute arising from the agreement

➡ **Entire agreement** — states that the license agreement is *the* agreement so that there is no confusion as to which prior discussions and written documents form part of it

➡ **Amendments** — states that any changes to the agreement be in writing and signed

➡ **Waiver** — allows either party to waive some but not all of the clauses in the agreement while the remainder of the agreement remains in effect

➡ **Independent parties** — states that the agreement does not create a legal relationship (i.e., joint venture, partnership, etc.) between the parties

→ **Survival** — provides that certain clauses survive the termination of the agreement such as the warranties and indemnities

→ **Severability** — states that should part of the agreement be invalid, the remaining portions survive if possible

→ **Remedies** — provides for certain remedies should there be a breach of the agreement (remedies include lawsuits for monetary damages and court injunctions to stop an ongoing action which harms one of the parties to the agreement)

→ **Binding effect** — allows the agreement to benefit successors, administrators, heirs, affiliates, and assigns of the parties signing the agreement (assigns might be subject to approval by the licensor)

→ **Further assurances** — in rights-related agreements, ensures that the rights holder will sign any further documents (copyright registration forms, etc.) where necessary

→ **Notice** — states that notices be in writing and specifies how they should be delivered to the other party (sent by "snail mail" or by fax or email)

→ **Force majeure** — provides for suspension or termination of the agreement due to events beyond the control of either party

Beyond the License Agreement

Registering Licenses

In some jurisdictions, there are advantages to registering certain "grants of interest" or changes in ownership of a copyright work, or a part of the copyright in the work. In some countries, including Canada, the subsequent owner of a whole or part of a work protected by copyright may have priority over any other similar grantee of interest if that other interest has not been registered. For instance, if X and Y are both granted an interest in a work protected by copyright and only Y registers this interest, Y may have priority over X with respect to his rights in the work. This is something you might want to verify in your own country.

Till Death Do Us Part

Like "tangible" property, IP can be passed on, upon death, to other persons through a will. Generally, a person inheriting the physical property (like real estate, furniture, and jewelry) of an IP owner will also inherit the intangible rights of copyright if there is no specific mention of these rights.

An owner of IP who, upon his death, would like the copyright in some or all of his works to pass on to specific persons should specify this in his will. You might consider appointing a "copyright" executor, that is, someone with special knowledge in the area and someone who understands the IP owner's desires. It is important that the copyright executor be in a position that enables him to exercise the desires of the IP owner and is not in any position that may lead to a conflict of interest. For example, a publisher may be in an awkward position as an executor for a writer who publishes with that publisher's firm.

Rights in Future Works

In practical terms, assignments relating to future works often take place. For example, a writer may sign a contract with a publishing house for a yet unwritten book. The same is true with respect to music publishing contracts. In relation to e-rights, licensees may request the rights for all media whatsoever, whether currently existing or yet to be "invented." Owners of IP should think carefully about giving away such broad rights. For instance, an IP owner who wrote a book twenty years ago may still have the e-rights to that book, unless he signed an agreement at that time for the book to be published in any medium whatsoever, whether then existing or in the future, and thus already gave away his e-rights. If an IP owner is given an offer to assign future rights to a work, the IP owner should consider whether the sum of money is worth the value of "unknown" rights or whether he should retain those rights and negotiate for their use at a later date. Content owners must always keep in mind that each right has a value attached to it. Persons obtaining e-rights should, on the other hand, ensure that they have all the necessary rights to be able to create and distribute an electronic product.

Other Contractual Arrangements

The licensing and sublicensing of rights discussed in this chapter is only one type of contractual relationship into which you may enter. You might also need to enter into agreements for the development of products with developers of CD-ROMs, DVDs, or Web sites, agreements with distributors of products, with Internet and online service providers, with financial clearing centers (who may help collect online payments), and with rights collectives and agencies (discussed below under secondary e-rights). In all of these situations, whether there is a transfer of your IP or an arrangement relating to it, be aware of your rights and obligations and secure written confirmation of them.

What Your Agreement Should Contain

The clauses discussed above are examples of issues to address in a license agreement. When licensing IP, you will have to decide, based on the circumstances, what is the appropriate type of arrangement and how you should set this out in your agreement. At one extreme is a simple document identifying the parties, the works being used, the purpose of their use, length of use, payment, and the rights being licensed, a warranty that the works are in fact owned by the party who is licensing them, and signatures of both parties. At the other extreme may be a twenty-page agreement full of legal terminology. A discussion of what constitutes a valid agreement follows in chapter 9.

Tips and Traps

Depending on your perspective as a individual creator, print or electronic publisher, library, archive, museum, corporation, or new media entrepreneur, there are a number of tips to follow and traps to avoid in your license agreements. In one situation, you may be licensing the rights to your photographs, while in the next situation you may yourself be obtaining the rights to use someone's article, animation, or audio clip on your Web site. In other words, we are often on both sides of the table and must be aware of both sides. A word of advice is to follow your instincts and always keep in mind the use of the work being licensed and what other uses could be made of that work if you had further rights to it. More specific advice is offered in the following summary of a presentation I recently gave to an audience of museum workers. In other words, this is one perspective on tips and traps — the perspective of an institutional content owner — but it may shed some light on your licensing situation no matter what perspective you may have.

Tips & Traps	**Tips to Follow and Traps to Avoid in Licensing Museum Content**

Whether you're developing your museum policy on digital licensing or entering into negotiations and contractual arrangements, there are certain things to consider that may not necessarily be true when licensing print and other nondigital rights. Digital licensing is a unique breed. But it is also a breed without many precedents or industry standards. My perspective today is a practical one. I'm here to provide you with tips on what to do and what not to do when licensing museum content. Please be aware, however, that my presentation time is brief and only five of the many important issues are surveyed.

Defining the Content

Tip: Always carefully define what is covered by a license agreement and be specific. Put this in writing and if possible attach a sketch or photo of the work. Otherwise, it may be difficult later to determine exactly what in your collections is covered by the license agreement and what is not and therefore capable of further exploitation by you.

Trap: There are sometimes two different copyright works when an image is digitized. There may be copyright in the original image, as well as a separate copyright in the digitized image.[3] As a museum licensing digital content, you could license the digitized image while retaining the copyright in the underlying image and thereby be able to later profit from exploiting the underlying image. So avoid the trap of licensing both the rights in the underlying and digitized work (unless you obtain compensation for both).

Nature of Transfer

Tip: Never assign the digital rights in your collections, as that means that you are permanently giving them away. Rather, license those rights, preferably on a nonexclusive basis. That way, you can license them to others, again on a nonexclusive basis. Also, you do not have to license rights for the duration of copyright, and in fact some digital license agreements are quite short. I recently prepared an agreement for an online publisher in which he only wanted the digital rights for a one-month period.

Trap: Probably the worst type of licensing arrangement is where you have licensed your rights on an exclusive basis and the licensor is not exploiting those rights and you are therefore not being paid since payment is dependent upon exploitation. In such a case, you could be in "licensing limbo." You cannot exploit your own rights and you are not benefiting from someone else doing so. To avoid this situation, include a reversion of rights clause in which, for instance, the digital rights revert back to your museum if they are not exploited within a set period of time (e.g., two years).

Geographical Boundary

Tip: At the current time, digital rights for use on the Internet means global rights. However, this may not always be true. Technology may develop which divides the Internet into geographical areas. If you agree to worldwide licensing, state so. If you want it limited, for instance, only for works downloaded in, let's say, England, or you are creative enough to find some other ways of limiting the rights, add it to your agreement. And keep in mind that you can limit the rights by other means, such as language — for example, you could license works only in the English language and not grant translation rights into every language.

Trap: The larger the geographical boundary, the more you should ask to be paid for your rights. Worldwide rights will of course get more payment than North American or European rights. In many situations, it is best to license global rights to the same licensee provided you are duly compensated (though this may be more difficult with the unknown revenues currently associated with content on the Internet and may be easier for instance with respect to a product like a CD-ROM). In other words, do not try to limit global licensing of digital rights even though global licensing of nondigital rights is often not the norm (unless, of course, it is beneficial to you).

Division of Rights

Tip: Digital rights is a broad term that includes Internet rights, Web site rights, CD-ROM rights, database rights, online publishing rights, software rights, and many others. In some situations, it may make sense to divide the licensing of your digital rights and not to license them as a bundle under the general term of digital rights. Even if you want to license all of your digital rights, your agreement should set out a specific payment related to each use, for example, x amount of dollars for CD-ROM use, x amount of dollars for Web site use, x amount of dollars for internal digital archive use, etc.

Trap: Avoid licensing any of your digital rights for any media now existing or which may exist in the future. If you are intending to license your works for the Internet, have the agreement state that. This will ensure that your digitized collections are only used on the Internet and not in a new computer network which might be in existence two years from now.

Value and Payment

Tip: The value of digitized collections and any intellectual property is very much what the market will pay. The notion of licensing digital rights is relatively new, and as yet there are no such things as typical rates or industry standards. And there are not many precedents. My greatest tip here is to set up a network amongst museums to exchange information on the value of your digital rights, what rights you are licensing, in what manner, and at what costs. Over time, industry standards will begin to emerge.

Trap: Although digital rights are new, many think that they have or will have tremendous value. However, the reality is that at the current time, there may not be that much money being made from the exploitation of digital rights. In some situations, and not particularly in museum cases, I've heard of people not entering into digital license agreements because they were not being offered enough for their rights. As a suggestion, if your licensee is not able or willing to pay what you believe is the value of your digital rights, do not walk away. If the lump sum you're offered is too low, ask for a percentage of profits. If you're still unhappy, limit the duration of the license, or make sure it is nonexclusive, and for one or two digital rights and not all of them.

Secondary E-Rights: A Different Story

Lately, there has been a lot of discussion about licensing e-rights. Basically, there are two types of e-rights licensing: primary, when you are licensing your rights initially or solely for electronic media, and secondary, when you are licensing your rights for another medium (for instance, print), with e-rights as only a secondary right addressed in your agreement. As an example, you may license the right to a publisher to publish your book in a print format and the publisher may also, as a secondary right, want to include the book on a CD-ROM. Or you may be licensing only the e-rights to your work, as primary rights, to appear on a Web site. Different issues may require different weight, depending on which type of rights you are licensing.

Until fairly recently, e-rights were usually treated as secondary rights. This is no longer the case. Today and increasingly in the future, more and more works (like photographs, illustrations, music, videos, and text) are being created initially and primarily for CD-ROMS, Web sites, intranets, and e-zines.

If you are licensing your works only for electronic uses, the value and related terms and conditions for your e-rights will be determined based on the factors set out earlier in this and the previous chapter. However, there is an important further consideration if e-rights are being licensed *in addition to* other non e-rights. Some print magazine and newspaper publishers are asking for (and in some cases assuming that) e-rights are part of their licensing of print rights, and therefore creators are not receiving additional payment for the electronic uses. The buzz in the creative community is for creators not to sign any agreements in which licensees ask for e-rights *without additional payment.* Such contracts should be carefully examined and should be discussed with your professional association or a copyright lawyer. This is a very sensitive issue at an important time, when industry standards have not yet been set and poor precedents can lead to lack of compensation for you in the future. Various interest groups are discussing ways to ensure fair compensation to creators for the use of their e-rights.

It should be noted that, for some time now, book publishers have been licensing electronic rights when obtaining the rights to publish a print version of a book; however, unlike the situation mentioned above, book publishers usually offer a percentage of revenue earned from the sale of e-rights similar to other subsidiary rights they obtain, such as for audiotapes or anthology use or excerpts. For instance, an author of a print book might be offered 50 percent of the revenue earned by the print publisher from the e-rights sales. This percentage is negotiable.

In order to provide clarity in freelance situations, when licensing the use of your works, it's a good idea to stamp on each work and also on any covering letter the exact use to which you are agreeing and also to mention, where true, that the particular license does not include e-rights. One phrasing used in the freelance writing community in Canada to exclude e-rights is "first English Canadian serial rights in print only." Also, keep in mind that where you do license your e-rights, you are allowing the use of the work as is. Unless you allow your work to be adapted, the licensee of your e-rights may, for instance, scan your image, but may not morph or manipulate it.

Final Word

Licensing content for new media is new to everyone. Most of us are struggling with the nature and substance of these important and complicated contractual arrangements. In any licensing situation, you must examine your own perspectives and goals, as well as take into account the other party's, and tailor your negotiations and agreements to match your particular circumstances. Keep in mind that there is room for creativity in your license agreements.

As with all agreements, it is best to consult a lawyer before signing on the dotted line, as opposed to consulting one at a later stage when a dispute arises. A well-written license agreement will in many cases avoid disputes in the future. It will be a document you refer to again and again when questions arise during the course of your relationship, either as a licensor or licensee — and hopefully, it will provide you with answers.

End Notes

1. Although a complicated matter to set out in legal language, in some cases the nonexclusive licensing arrangement could be negotiated so that if certain minimum amounts of money are earned by the licensee from the nonexclusive arrangement, then there is an automatic conversion to an exclusive license, which would better protect the rights of the licensee and allow for greater revenues for him, which in turn could be shared with the content owner.

2. Lesley Ellen Harris, *Canadian Copyright Law*, 2nd ed. (Toronto: McGraw-Hill Ryerson, 1995), 100–101.

3. This is a debatable issue under U.S. copyright law.

CHAPTER 6

The Legal Protection of Digital Property

Oh, I forgot. You were sick the day they taught law at law school.

— Tom Cruise, in *A Few Good Men* (written by Aaron Sorkin)

We've now examined what kinds of IP have current, potential, and future value, how to place a dollar amount on that value, and terms and conditions relating to the licensing of your IP. Prior to going out in the marketplace to make some money from your digital property, it's important to understand the underlying basis for its value. This chapter gives a quick tour through copyright law, the area of IP law that most predominantly protects your digital property.

Building Your Confidence

Most people know more about copyright law than they think. Below are three quizzes to help determine your knowledge level and to build your "knowledge confidence." You probably won't stumble too much in the Beginner's Quiz, and chances are you'll enjoy debating some of the questions in the Advanced Quiz. If you can answer all the questions in the Genius Quiz, you might want to consider law school, or perhaps applying for a job in your country's copyright office.

Beginner's Quiz

1. May you publish someone else's manuscript without their permission?

2. May you photocopy an entire book?

3. Do you recognize the following symbol: ©

4. If you purchase computer software, may you make unlimited copies of it?

5. Is it legal to tape a live Rolling Stones concert?

6. Can anyone use the Mickey Mouse character in any manner they wish?

7. Can you go to jail for copyright infringement?

8. Is it legal to record a television program with your VCR?

9. Who owns copyright in your work if you are an employee?

10. Who owns copyright in your work if you are self-employed and prepared the work for a client?

11. Are creators of copyright works allowed to assign or license their works to others (e.g., publishers, producers, developers) in exchange for money?

12. Do copyright laws provide you with a right to prevent major modifications to your work?

Advanced Quiz

1. Can you publish a collection of letters sent to you?

2. Can you photocopy half of a book for personal use?

3. If the © symbol does not appear on a work, does that mean that it is not protected by copyright?

4. If you purchase computer software, is it legal to make one copy of it for your desktop computer and another copy for your laptop computer?

5. Is it legal to perform your own rendition of a Rolling Stones song in a bar?

6. Is it legal to incorporate a parody of the Mickey Mouse character in your own comic strip?

7. If you give someone permission to use your copyright work, must that permission be in writing?

8. Can you show a rented video to a group of boy scouts? How about in a movie theatre where you collect one dollar from each viewer?

9. Are confidential information and trade secrets protected by copyright?

10. Can you photocopy an article from the newspaper for classroom use?

11. Do authors get paid copyright royalties when their books are borrowed from libraries? What if their books are sold in secondhand stores?

12. Are there mechanisms or remedies in copyright laws to protect you if your original work of art is destroyed?

Genius Quiz

1. If you own a painting, do you also own the copyright in it?

2. If the Mona Lisa were still protected by copyright, would it be illegal to paint a moustache on her face?

3. Is it legal to photocopy an article downloaded off the Internet?

4. When radio stations play music on the air, are they exempt from copyright restrictions because they are providing "free advertising"?

5. Do Canada and the U.S. have the same copyright laws?

6. Do all member countries of the European Economic Community have the same copyright laws?

7. Is there an international copyright law to cover international copyright infringements?

8. Are governments bound by copyright laws?

9. Are cyberspace and the Internet subject to copyright laws?

10. Does copyright inhibit free speech and access to information?

11. How do a particular country's copyright laws apply to a global network like the Internet?

12. Are copyright laws necessary on the Internet?

Sorry, this chapter doesn't provide the answers to these quizzes. It does, however, provide you with the underlying principles of copyright laws so that you can answer these questions yourself.

Famous Copyright Cases

Even if you don't know the answers to *all* of the above questions, you might be familiar with some of the more prominent court cases involving copyright matters. Some of these cases are summarized below.

Case: George Harrison was sued for his song "My Sweet Lord" for allegedly infringing the copyright in "He's So Fine" (composed by Ronald Mack and performed by The Chiffons).

Decision: The U.S. court decided that George Harrison did infringe the copyright of "He's So Fine" even though it was unconscious copying. The court said, "His subconscious knew it already had worked in a song his conscious did not remember. . . ."[1]

Have some fun: Go to the Copyright Web site: (*http://www.benedict.com/*), where you can hear both songs and compare them for yourself.

Case: A television station in France was sued in order to prevent it from showing a colorized version of film director John Huston's 1950 film *The Asphalt Jungle*.

Decision: The French court (on November 23, 1988) upheld an injunction prohibiting the French television station from showing the colorized version.

Case: Canadian artist Michael Snow instituted a court action when the Toronto Eaton Centre tied ribbons around the necks of the sixty geese in his sculpture *Flight Stop* as a Christmas decoration.

Decision: The court held that the attachment of the ribbons to the sculpture was prejudicial to the artist's honor or reputation and ordered that the ribbons be removed. The court said, "the plaintiff is adamant in his belief that his naturalistic composition has been made to look ridiculous by the addition of ribbons and suggests it is not unlike dangling earrings from the Venus de Milo."

Newspaper Headings

Court cases are not the only way copyright issues have been brought to the forefront. Here is a quote from a newspaper article that may ring a bell:

> *Some artists don't have control over their songs' use. The Beatles' "Revolution" was used in a 1987 Nike commercial without the Fab Four's permission. The group's publishing library is owned by Michael Jackson, who sold the tune to Nike, which also purchased the rights to the Beatles' own version of the song from units of Capitol Industries-EMI.[2]*

Obviously, copyright issues do surround many aspects of our lives, whether or not we realize it. The remainder of this chapter provides you with some specific knowledge about copyright law.

Copyright Takes the Lead

For people working in the digital world, copyright has become the primary concern amongst the various areas of intellectual property law.

> *Copyright is the Cinderella of the law. Her rich old sisters, Franchises and Patents, long crowded her*

into the chimney corner. Suddenly the Fairy God-
mother, Invention, endowed her with mechanical
and electrical devices as magical as the pumpkin
coach and the mice footmen. Now she whirls
through the mad mazes of a glamorous ball.[3]

From the Printing Press to the Internet

Interestingly, the very reason for the existence of copyright laws
is the reason why they are taking the limelight as a topic of discussion on the Internet amongst content owners and users. And
it is the same reason they will continue to be a predominant area
of IP law in the twenty-first century. Technology. Copyright laws
have always been linked closely to technology and the relatively
new and easy means of exploiting creative works. Copyright
laws date back to 1476, when the first printing press was introduced into England, and the genesis of the need to control unauthorized reproduction of creations. By 1534, no one could publish
without a license. In 1709, the Parliament of England passed the
first copyright statute, the *Statute of Anne.*

The World's First Copyright Statute

The purpose of the *Statute of Anne* was to reward publishers and
printers for their efforts (though the Act was later construed as
protecting authors) while recognizing the public's need to access
these publications, in an attempt to balance the needs of creators,
publishers, and consumers of copyright materials. The underlying principles of the *Statute of Anne* have remained the model for
modern copyright laws (for example, in the United States, Canada,
and the United Kingdom) and international copyright instruments. In fact, the same principles intended to protect creators
have again and again proven flexible enough to embrace each
new form of creativity to come into existence.

We now have both national copyright laws worldwide and international copyright conventions which not only apply to print

books but to new technologies of the nineteenth century (audio recordings and photographs), technologies of the twentieth century (satellite transmissions, videotapes, photocopiers, computer programs, and now transmission on the Internet), and undoubtedly to the technologies of the twenty-first century, whatever they may happen to be.

A Human Right

It is interesting to note that the role of copyright is much broader than an economic one and is treated in a variety of lights. For instance, Article 27 of the Universal Declaration of Human Rights states: "Everyone has the right to protection of the moral and material interests resulting from any scientific, literary or artistic production of which he is the author."

How Copyright Laws Work

Copyright laws around the world provide copyright creators and owners with certain rights, which they may then exchange for compensation, usually in the form of money. The amount of compensation (or money) is determined by the marketplace — just like when you put your car or house up for sale. You generally know what it's worth, or at least what to ask for, but then you have to entertain offers, and often enter negotiations until the exact price to be paid is agreed upon. Copyright operates in much the same way. The major difference is that when you look at a house, you already know *how* to determine its value. You know that the location of it is important, as is the material of which it is made, and its size, and perhaps what the purchaser will do with the house. You know that you probably cannot build an addition to the house without obtaining the proper building permits (or permissions) and that if you make too much noise when you have your housewarming party, there's a good chance that the police will show up uninvited at the party.

But what do you know about your copyright-protected works? Take the example of a book manuscript. If you want to sell the IP in your book, are you really aware of what you're selling? You're probably certain that you can sell the right to publish the book, but what about translating it, or transmitting parts or all of it on the Internet? And what if you as its author want to use a pseudonym? And if the story is based on your grandmother's life, who owns the copyright to the story, or to letters your grandmother received from your grandfather? And what if you used the computer at work to type the manuscript — does that affect the ownership of its copyright? And for how long do you have these copyright rights? And what happens if someone publishes your book without your permission? And can you put the book on the Internet?

As you can see, you'll need to understand the nature of copyright protection in order to be able to place a value on a copyright work and to negotiate a fair price for your digital property. So set out below is an explanation of the basic principles found in most copyright laws around the world. The specifics of each country's copyright laws do vary, and depending on what you're doing with your copyright works, you should research and review the copyright laws in the jurisdiction(s) where your work is created and distributed, and obtain proper legal advice where necessary.

Property Rights in a Creation

> *Only one thing is impossible to God: to find any sense in any copyright law on the planet.*
> — Mark Twain

There are two very important concepts that must be appreciated for a full understanding of copyright law: the concept of how copyright protection relates to ideas, and the concept of protecting "intangible" property.

Copyright Protection and Ideas

As you know, you can't copyright an idea . . .
— Michael Douglas, in *Fatal Attraction* (written by James Dearden)

IDEAS ARE NOT PROTECTED BY COPYRIGHT LAW. This cannot be overstressed. What the law protects is the *expression* of ideas. This is based on the notion that ideas are part of the public domain and that no one can have a monopoly in them. There is also no copyright protection in concepts, information, facts, history, or news events. Copyright protects the *words or expression* used in a book to describe something, like how to build a bicycle — anyone may, without permission, build a bicycle by following the instructions in the book.

What this also means is that there can be copyright in two works expressing the same idea since it is the original expression of the idea which is protected by copyright. For example, two people may independently make sketches of the same tree, each sketch being protected by copyright and neither of them violating the copyright in the other one.

Some country's copyright laws are very explicit in stating this basic concept. For example, the U.S. Copyright Act states, "In no case does copyright protection for an original work of authorship extend to any idea, procedure, process, system, method of operation, concept, principle, or discovery, regardless of the form in which it is described, explained, illustrated, or embodied in such work." The new Copyright Treaty adopted in Geneva in December 1996 states, "Copyright protection extends to expressions and not to ideas, procedures, methods of operation or mathematical concepts as such."

Intangible versus Tangible Property Rights

When you have a creation, you have two property rights in this creation. First, you have the right in the physical property, in the creation itself. Second, you have the right in the intangible property, attracting certain rights which govern the use of the creation. Copyright protects this intangible right. Thus, if you own a book, you may read it, display it on your coffee table, and even lend it to a friend. However, you may not do anything which only the copyright owner has the exclusive right to do. For example, by virtue of owning the physical book, you may not reproduce or translate it or scan it into your computer.

What's Protected by Copyright?

Broadly speaking, the copyright laws in any one country protect a variety of creations. Using somewhat statutory language (that is, the language found in a country's laws), copyright protects literary, artistic, dramatic, and musical works, as well as sound recordings, videos, and films. These broad terms include poems, articles, fiction and nonfiction writing, computer software and games, CD-ROMs, DVDs, interactive and multimedia works, Web sites, photographs, digital images, translations, speeches, architectural plans, paintings, computer-assisted drawings, music videos, and films. As you can see, copyright protects most of the content we create and use.

For purposes of this book, the terms *IP, content, works*, and *copyright works* are used somewhat interchangably to refer to the types of creations protected by copyright law.

The arts and entertainment worlds are copyright-based industries. An artist creates a copyright-protected painting and a screenwriter creates a copyright-protected script. A film producer obtains the rights to a script and turns it into a film, also a copyright-protected work. Other elements of the film will be protected by copyright, like the music and soundtrack. The computer software industry is purely based on the creation of copyright-protected works — the object and source code in computer software. Those in schools and workplaces are constantly creating and using copyright materials, whether it's a video or school newspaper or corporate newsletter.

What's Not Protected by Copyright, but Protected by Other Areas of IP?

I read somewhere that if you get an original idea, you can rest assured it will occur to at least 5000 other people simultaneously. However, that amazing statistic went on to say that only two of those 5000 original thinkers will have the initiative and opportunity to do anything. So it narrows very quickly to a contest between you and one other person out there who may be thinking he or she has it all to themselves.

— Howard Goldstein, *Micro Publishing News*[4]

Copyright is one of the five traditional areas of intellectual property law, which includes patents, trademarks, industrial designs, and confidential information/trade secrets. Each type of IP protects a different kind of creation or a different aspect of a creation, and each type provides its own special set of rules of protection. Patents protect things like inventions, new medicines, machines, communications systems, energy sources, and electric can openers. Trademarks protect words, names, symbols, pictures, logos, designs, or shapes of goods (for instance, the words Coca-Cola or Microsoft). Industrial designs protect an original shape, pattern, or ornamentation applied to a useful article like a pattern on wallpaper or the shape of a table. Confidential information/trade secrets protect concepts, ideas, and factual information, such as the concept for a Web site or idea for a computer program or television show. Further, there is an area of the law that protects "chips," the tiny electronic devices found in VCRs and washing machines and robots. A work or creation can be protected by more than one area of IP.

How About Protection in Other Countries?

There is no one international copyright law. Each country has its own copyright laws. However, the citizens of many countries are protected by copyright law in other countries based on the principle of national treatment. Under the Berne Convention, the leading international copyright treaty, each of the over one hundred countries that belong to it automatically provides citizens from other member countries at least the same copyright protection it provides its own citizens. For example, a Canadian creator is entitled to the same copyright protection in the United States as any U.S. citizen. Further, a British photographer is entitled to the same copyright protection in the United States as any U.S. photographer. Once copyright protection is secured in one Berne country, protection is automatic in all other Berne countries. There are no prerequisite formalities for the protection, such as registering a work, or marking it with the copyright symbol. The protection extends to the rights of the creator as well as remedies available for the violation of these rights. Information on the Berne Convention and a list of its members is available from the World Intellectual Property Organization (WIPO) site (*http://www.wipo.int/*).

Countries who are not members to Berne may be protected by the other international copyright convention, the Universal Copyright Convention (UCC), or through other agreements between various countries. A copy of the UCC is available at *http://www.tufts.edu/departments/fletcher/multi/texts/UNTS13444.txt*.

In addition, there are two new WIPO international copyright treaties dealing with digital media which are discussed in chapter 10. Both treaties are reprinted in the appendices.

Trade Agreements

The push for the international distribution of IP is evident when we examine the growth of IP in international trade agreements.

Until recently, international copyright relations were through international copyright conventions and bilateral agreements. However, in the past several years, a number of international trade agreements have included provisions for IP. These trade agreements are the Canada-United States Free Trade Agreement (FTA), the North American Free Trade Agreement (NAFTA), and the Agreement on Trade Related Aspects of Intellectual Property Rights (TRIPs), which was part of the Uruguay Round of the General Agreement on Tariffs and Trade (GATT). Countries that signed the GATT are members of the World Trade Organization (WTO).

IP is included in trade agreements in order to strengthen intellectual property rights around the world and to encourage foreign investment by combating piracy, to enhance standards for the protection of copyright around the world, and to strengthen the enforcement of rights both internally and at the borders.

What does all this mean to new media entrepreneurs? It means that with greater international protection of IP, there are further secure markets and incentives to disseminate their IP in more countries around the world.

How Does One Obtain Copyright Protection?

In many countries, copyright protection is automatic from the moment a work is created (e.g., in a "fixed" form such as on paper, your computer hard drive, or a computer disk). This means that no registration or deposit with a government copyright office may be required in order to have copyright protection. There are, however, *voluntary* government registration systems where copyright owners can register their works, thereby gaining entitlement to certain benefits, especially in cases of copyright infringements of the works.

In some countries, including Canada, an additional and/or alternative mode of "registration" is mailing a copy of the work to oneself by registered mail; note that this may not be acceptable in the United States.

It should be noted that Berne member countries must all provide automatic copyright protection.

Does a Work Need a © Symbol?

© Jane Doe 1997

Similar to copyright registration, use of the copyright symbol is not mandatory in Berne countries, though it is mandatory in countries that are members of the UCC, as discussed above.

Whether or not the marking is mandatory for protection in a particular country, it is a good idea to mark a work with the copyright symbol, author's name, and date of publication as a reminder to others that copyright exists in the work. And it can help people locate and contact the copyright owner to obtain permission prior to using a work.

The copyright notice should be clearly placed in a manner and location best suited to alert the user of the work in question to the fact that copyright subsists in the work. This can vary depending on the type of work involved. For a Web site, suitable locations for the copyright notice may be on the homepage, which Net surfers first see upon entering the Web site, or on a special notice page which appears when a surfer clicks on a specific icon.[5] As a general rule, place the notice in a manner and location that gives reasonable notice of the claim of copyright, so that it appears in a conspicuous position on a work and will not be missed by a casual observer.

The year to include in a copyright notice should be the year of first publication, or the year in which substantial revisions to a work occurred. For constantly evolving Web sites, the year in the notice would be updated whenever more than trivial revisions or additions are made to the site. While earlier years can remain as part of the notice, the date of the latest substantial revisions must be included. If only one year is to appear in the notice, it should be the oldest year; or, in other words, the year associated with the oldest elements in the work. It is best to err on the side of omitting newer years as opposed to omitting older years. Alternatively, you could include a range of years (e.g., 1995–1997), starting from the date of the oldest elements in the work and ending with the date of the newest elements in the work.

The question of the proper year, or years, to use in a copyright notice can be problematical, depending on the type of work involved and the frequency of amendments or revisions to it. However, these issues are by no means unique to computer software or Web sites. Any work that is regularly updated, such as a dictionary, almanac, or encyclopedia, contains items dating from many different years. At least one copyright notice will appear in such a work, and perhaps more, each containing many different years.

How Long Does Copyright Last?

Until recently, the general term of copyright protection in most countries was *life-plus-fifty* — that is, lasting for the life of the author plus fifty years after his death (often until the calendar year end of his death). For example, an author who died on February 1, 1950, has copyright protection in her works until December 31, 2000.

However, certain countries, primarily European ones, have lengthened this duration to *life-plus-seventy*. It will be interesting to watch whether other countries extend the term of protection, and many discussions are already taking place on this issue.

What Does "Public Domain" Mean?

Once copyright expires, the work is in the public domain and can be used without obtaining permission or paying a fee. Images, text, and music in the public domain can be freely used, even in a digital format. In the film and other industries, public domain works are often referred to as "PD."

Who Owns a Copyright Work?

This is an extremely important point from the perspective of the alleged owner of a copyright work as well as from the perspective of someone purchasing IP. And, unfortunately, ownership is not always clear on the surface. If you've heard the expression "chain of title," ownership is what it refers to. For example, who owns the work in a computer program written by a freelance programmer, adapted by an employee, then licensed to a sister company, who then converts it to another computer language? To establish the chain of title, you have to begin by examining the nature of the relationship between the freelance programmer and the company who hired the programmer (and in the ideal world, there will be a contract spelling out who owns the copyright), and then examine each subsequent situation. Not an easy task. And not always a task that results in clear, straightforward answers.

Often the creator of a copyright work is the first owner of copyright in it; however, this would be subject to the copyright laws in any one jurisdiction as well as the particular circumstances. For instance, if the work were made in the course of employment, it might belong to the employer, or it if were commissioned, it might be owned by the person who ordered it. There is a "work-for-hire" provision in U.S. law that covers some of these situations and should be carefully examined should a work be made in an employment or commissioned situation in the United States or with a U.S. company.

The Rights of a Copyright Owner

Copyright is, literally, the "right to copy." Copyright includes a "bundle" of rights, include reproducing (e.g., photocopying, photographing, scanning into a computer), performing in public (e.g., at a concert), publishing in print (e.g., in a book) or in an electronic format (e.g., on the Internet), publicly displaying, adapting (e.g., a book into a movie script), translating, publicly communicating, and broadcasting. Only the owner of copyright may do these things with a creation or authorize others to do so.

Electronic Rights

Electronic rights, or e-rights, are part of the "bundle" of rights belonging to a copyright owner. They are dealt with under a separate heading here for two reasons. First, e-rights are relatively new and are not as established in copyright laws as, for example, the right to publish a work in print. Second, the existence of e-rights is one of the reasons why you would even purchase a book in print called *Digital Property* and why copyright works have become a major IP asset.

So what are electronic rights? E-rights are referred to by a variety of names, including digital rights, database rights, multimedia rights, interactive rights, Web site rights, Internet rights, and CD-ROM rights. E-rights include reproduction, public performance, adaptation, broadcast, and all the other rights specified in copyright laws. E-rights, like many other rights in copyright, may not be specifically referred to in the copyright statute of your country — but you can still establish ownership of them and therefore license them, and include them in your contracts dealing with the licensing of your copyright works. This topic was explored in chapter 5, "Selling and Licensing Digital Property."

Moral Rights

My personal belief is, of course, that no one should ever be able to tamper with any artist's work in any medium against the artist's will.

— Woody Allen

If there is a sexy side to copyright, moral rights is it. And with digital manipulations and morphing, it has become the focus of greater attention.

In copyright law, moral rights protect the personality of an "author." Here are some examples where moral rights protected artists in a variety of circumstances. On March 18, 1992, hours before a trial was to begin in Los Angeles, renowned muralist Kent Twitchell agreed to a settlement of $175,000 over the destruction of his Los Angeles mural *The Old Woman of the Freeway*. Appearing on the wall of a building, the mural was first half covered by the building of a new parking structure and then destroyed, which under California state law is a violation of an artist's moral right.

On November 23, 1988, a French court upheld an injunction prohibiting a French television station from showing a colorized version of John Huston's 1950 film *The Asphalt Jungle*. The work was originally filmed in black and white, and John Huston, the film's director, did not authorize the colorization of the film. Huston and the court felt that this violated his right of integrity.

On April 29, 1983, playwright Sharon Pollock was awarded an interlocutory injunction in a Canadian court to ban the broadcast of a television version of her play *Blood Relations*, which she felt distorted the play's interpretation of the life of accused Massachusetts axe-murderer Lizzie Borden. In this case, Ms. Pollock asserted her moral right to prevent a distortion from the adaptation of her work which could be prejudicial to her honor and reputation.

In copyright law parlance, moral rights protect the "personality" of an author, the author's honor and reputation. Moral rights are distinct from the economic or copyright rights of reproduction, adaptation, public performance, telecommunication, and so on, and do not have the underlying purpose of monetarily compensating authors for the use of their creations.

The scope of protection provided by moral rights varies from country to country. In France, the moral rights are very strong: "the author shall enjoy the right to respect for his name, his authorship, and his work." This right is "attached" to the person and is "perpetual, inalienable and imprescriptible." The U.S. Copyright Act provides limited moral rights (mostly for visual artists) and asserts that contract, slander, defamation, trademark, and unfair competition law together protect *all* creators as required by the Berne Convention. In Canada, an author has the moral rights of paternity and integrity and the additional right of association. In the United Kingdom, authors enjoy the rights of paternity and integrity.

In certain countries, like the United States, moral rights are not always specified in contractual arrangements; however, it is possible that with new media, moral rights take a more prominent role in contractual arrangements in the United States, as they do in other countries.

Definition of Moral Rights

There is no one definitive definition of moral rights. One often-quoted definition of moral rights is that found in the Berne Convention: "Independently of the author's economic rights, and even after the transfer of said rights, the author shall have the right to claim authorship of the work and to object to any distortion, mutilation or other modification of, or other derogatory action in relation to, the said work, which would be prejudicial to his honour or reputation." From this definition stem two of the basic components of moral rights: the right of paternity and the right of integrity.

Paternity

The right of paternity, or the right to respect for one's name (as worded in French law), is the author's right to assert that he is the creator of a work. This right allows an author to place his name on, for instance, a book, digitized image, or computer program. The right may also protect authors who prefer to remain anonymous or to use a pseudonym.

Integrity

The right of integrity protects an author from harmful substantial changes being made to a work. For example, it prevents several chapters being cut from a book, the colorization of a black-and-white film, and the manipulation of a digital photograph. Generally, the author can prevent any substantial changes if prejudicial to his honor or reputation, a matter which a court of law would decide on a case-by-case basis.

There is a fine line between the moral right of integrity and the economic right of adaptation. In order to adapt a work — for instance, a book into a screenplay — one must clear the economic right of adaptation from the author of the book. However, if the right of integrity exists in that country, notwithstanding that the adaptation rights have been cleared, the adaptor must maintain the integrity of the book and make sure that any substantial changes in the adaptation are not prejudicial to the honor or reputation of the writer of the book. Nonsubstantial changes which do not harm the reputation of the author are generally not protected by the right of integrity.

Disclosure

Another moral right is the right of disclosure. This right is based on the principle that only the author has the right to disclose his work. The author has the right to decide whether the creation should be made public and whether he finds it sufficiently satisfactory to be submitted to public judgment. This right could, for example, prevent a creditor in a bankruptcy situation from seizing a manuscript and publishing it without the author's consent.

It would also allow a dramatist to undergo a reading without being obliged to stage the play to the public at large.

Reconsidering or Withdrawing

A fourth moral right is the right to reconsider or the right of withdrawal. This right allows an author to correct a "published" work or to withdraw it definitively from circulation.

Association

Another moral right is the right of association. For instance, in Canada an author has the right to prevent the use of his work "with a product, service, cause, or institution" where prejudicial to his honor or reputation. An example would be an art exhibit sponsored by a tobacco company where the artist's reputation rides on the fact that she is a nonsmoking advocate.

Other Rights

It is arguable that another moral right be the right to regain control of a work that is not used (e.g., not published or distributed), so that the copyright owner can "regain" control of rights that are not being exploited.

Although some or all of the moral rights may not be protected by a copyright statute, you may be able to include them in your license agreements.

The Duration of Moral Rights

In countries that grant moral rights, some specify that moral rights last for the same duration as the economic rights (Netherlands, Luxembourg, Canada). The debate regarding the duration of moral rights generally focuses on whether the rights should cease upon the death of the author. Countries like France, Italy, and Mexico have moral rights which are perpetual. However, French courts have held that the right to reconsider or to withdraw is such a personal right that it can only be exercised by the author him or herself.

Neighboring and Performers' Rights

Neighboring rights protect the rights of performers (actors, singers, and the like), record producers, and broadcasters. Neighboring rights are rights akin to copyright, but are distinct from copyright. Whereas copyright can be described as those rights granted to creators of copyright works, neighboring rights are rights granted to certain "users" of those copyright works. For example, copyright protects the composer of a song, whereas neighboring rights would protect the performer of the song. Another way of putting it is that a performer performs music to produce a "neighboring" work called a performer's performance. Neighboring rights can sometimes be obtained through contractual agreements.

Neighboring rights exist in some countries and constitute another area to watch for, as they are being added to the laws of more countries and are the subject of one of the new WIPO treaties discussed elsewhere in this book.

What Can Be Freely Copied?

Depending on the specifics of the copyright legislation in any one country, most uses of copyright materials require the permission of the copyright owner. Some countries, however, have exceptions for specific uses, including personal use, as well as for specific users like those in schools, libraries, and archives. An exception is an act which is allowed by the law and thus does not violate copyright. An exception means that a consumer does not have to clear permission to copy a work nor does he have to pay for that copy. Although exceptions limit the rights of copyright owners regarding the use of their works, they exist to balance the interests of owners and users (like educators, librarians, and others) who want to access these materials at reasonable costs. To meet this balance, certain copyright legislations provide exceptions for specific user groups.

Transferring Rights

The owner of a copyright work may license (give temporary permission) or assign (give permanent permission) to others to use or own that copyright work. The fee for the use of a copyright work is usually a matter to be negotiated between the copyright owner and user of the right(s).

Final Word

Copyright law is a complicated area. However, as a creator and content owner or someone using and acquiring IP, it is important that you have an understanding of this area. It is the underlying basis of protection in your works and is often what provides your work with value, from which you can make money. Take the time to understand how copyright law works. Join the many discussions at seminars and conferences, and on the Internet, to follow how it evolves and is applied to digital property. And now, you can turn your mind to your new media opportunities.

End Notes

1. *Bright Tunes Music Corp.* v. *Harrisongs Music, Ltd.* 420 F.Supp. 177 (1976).

2. Kevin Goldman, "A Few Rockers Give Ad Makers No Satisfaction," *Wall Street Journal*, 25 August 1995, p. B4.

3. Zachariah Chafee, "Reflections on the Law of Copyright," 45 *Columbia Law Review* 719.

4. Howard Goldstein, "Sour Grapes and Sweet Lemons," *Micro Publishing News*, September 1994, p. 49.

5. It is probably not necessary to include a copyright notice on every page of the Web site, though this may be something to discuss with your lawyer.

CHAPTER 7
New Media Opportunities

Audiences don't know that a writer writes the script; they think the actors make it up as they go along.

— William Holden (as Joe Gillis), in *Sunset Boulevard* (written by Charles Brackett, D.M. Marshman Jr., and Billy Wilder)

It's a different economy and job market out there. It's different from what we grew up with and different from what our parents and grandparents knew. And chances are, the changes are not temporary. Whether we realize it or not, we are living during pivotal times. What the next generation will call history and the Information Revolution is what the 1990s and early twenty-first century is about — and it is our lives. We are in the midst of a transformation from an industrial society to an information society, facing the same sort of upheaval our ancestors faced approximately one hundred years ago when we transformed from an agricultural to an industrial economy.

The Battle of the Content

In 1993, when QVC and Viacom battled for control of Paramount and its archive of classic films, it became clear that both companies believe the future lies in ownership of "content."

— Ann Okerson, *Scientific American*[1]

So far, little discussion in this book has focused on the companies who are acquiring the content of others — and who may want your content. As well as being potential sources of revenue, these companies may act as models or examples to provide you with ideas for starting your own company. Since the late 1980s, investors in the multimedia marketplace have been quietly acquiring e-rights and purchasing IP, with a view that this would be the content to fill the I-way, even though we were not then certain what the I-way would look like and how the content would be used. The only thing known for sure was that content was necessary.

Time-Warner, for example, has been acquiring e-rights to material for years, and a major reason behind the QVC-Viacom bidding war for Paramount was because the winner would control the Paramount movie/television inventory and the IP assets of one of the country's largest publishers, Simon and Schuster. Bill Gates has been busy acquiring shares of smaller software and multimedia developers, not to mention the rights to images in museums around the world (see below under "Libraries and Museums"). Gates also owns shares in companies like Dorling Kindersley, a major international book packager. The business press is full of stories of companies such as CBS, QVC, Blockbuster Video, the telephone companies, and so on, looking to acquire or merge with other companies to ensure they have valuable IP inventories.

These are just some of the many examples but they highlight, among other things, the need for content as well as the importance of collaboration and cooperative arrangements amongst the various media of broadcasting, film, print, and others, a trend that underlies the new media industry.

The 500-Channel Universe

The battle for content is just beginning. As the means for the distribution of IP continue to expand, the need for content grows and, from today's vantage point, almost seems insatiable. Take the promise we first heard about three or four years ago that allured us to the possibility of 500 television channels beamed directly into our dens and bedrooms. The media focus on mega-channel television was intense, but now it has shifted to the Internet. As the centre of our media universe, the Internet is increasingly expected to supplement and in certain circumstances even replace our stereos and radios and newspapers and televisions and books. Existing content which once filled the traditional media, as well as new content, will continue to be available through the Net. We require old, new, modified, and value-added content, and we need it in large quantities in order to fill the limitless numbers of "channels" existing and soon to be existing on the Internet.

Who's Profiting So Far?

So who is making money on the digital frontier? Widerness guides and hired guns.

— Seth Schiesel, *New York Times*[2]

The new media is attracting people to the same extent as the gold rushes of the nineteenth century, and often with the same result — many are going home empty-handed. Of those who rushed to find their gold, the entrepreneurs who sold pickaxes and blue jeans profited more than those who dug for gold. Similarly, many of the winners so far of the content gold rush have been conference organizers, magazines, and headhunters. This fact has caused many commentators to suggest that the potential for great profits to be reaped from the Internet is overrated and perhaps nonexistent. However, as with anything, timing and preparation is key. Even a good comedian cannot pull off a great joke without the right timing.

When the U.S. Defense Department launched Arpanet, the precursor to the Internet, in 1969, it rested in the domain of sophisticated users, primarily scientists, academics, and government specialists, for purposes of research and sharing information. When graphical interfaces became popular only recently, via the World Wide Web, the Internet became an open door for the general public. Its purpose is much the same — research and sharing information — only amongst a much larger audience. However, with the growth of the Web, businesses began to see new opportunities. It is amazing that only three years ago (1994), two U.S. immigration lawyers were "spammed" for using the Internet for commercial purposes.[3] Look at how far we have come in three years.

Skills

Working or making a living in what may be called the digital economy or an "information-obsessed" economy entails two shifts in the mind of the income earner. The first shift relates to skills and the second to the nature of that income or compensation for one's work.

So what kinds of skills are important in an information-obsessed economy? Broadly put, we need skills that allow us to gather, administer, analyze, and put into practical use that information, to package, market, and make accessible that information. Information by itself has little value. So we need skills that allow us to make valuable use of that information.

Old Positions, New Skills

There are at least two categories of what I call "information skills." The first category is *old positions that require new skills*. For example, a person formerly in the position of a secretary might retrain to become a data entry person, or the person responsible for digitizing information. An accountant whose work once entailed ledger entries and balances and reconciliations, which are now more quickly and accurately done by a computer program, can now spend her billable time analyzing the end results (rather than producing them) and providing practical advice to increase the productivity and revenue of her clients. But first that accountant must learn and understand the computer software upon which she makes her analysis, thus maintaining and improving her "old" position with new skills.

New Positions, New Skills

> JOE GILLIS: *You used to be in pictures. You used to be big.*
>
> NORMA DESMOND: *I am big. It's the pictures that got small.*
>
> — *Sunset Boulevard* (written by Charles Brackett, D.M. Marshman Jr., and Billy Wilder)

The second category of information skills is *new positions that require some old skills and some new skills* (which some might interpret to mean, there are no new skills, only new applications of old skills). A good example is the person who designs Web sites. Obviously, the design of a Web site is a skill that is as new as Web sites are new to our world. However, when you look at who is designing Web sites, for the most part it is not people coming out of college or university with a degree in Web site designing. It is people who "fell" into Web designing because of their interest in the Internet, or because they literally "played" with certain design-aiding computer software to help out a friend or create their own family or business Web site, or because they have a background in design, and digital media like the Internet are an important market for any design skills. Most Web site developers are people who learned their skills on the job!

Nature of Income

Earning a living in the information economy means new types of income payment, which in many cases will be radically different from a traditional salary. For instance, income may not necessarily be limited to monetary wages. We are seeing many computer software companies that already provide reasonable salaries also giving their employees stock options in the company. These options can have tremendous value if the company does well.

But stock options is only one example. IP industries traditionally have not consisted of salaried positions. Fiction writers, for example, are rarely if ever given a salary. Writers write their books ("properties") on speculation ("on spec"), or more established ones write outlines, which they then try to sell by themselves or through their literary agent to book publishers. Generally, writers will earn two types of monetary payment for that book. First, they will earn an advance. This advance is the money they receive before the book is published, at the time of signing the publishing contract and/or submitting the completed manuscript to the publisher. The advance "buys" the author time, or provides him with an income to cover her expenses while she is writing the book. It is also an advance against further payments to the writer.

The writer will also earn royalties, a percentage of the moneys earned from book sales, often 10 to 15 percent of the cover price of the book (depending on what the writer or her agent negotiates for that particular book deal). The advance is usually made against those royalties, which means that first the book sales have to go beyond the writer's advance before the writer will be entitled to any royalties. So if an author is given an advance of $10,000 against royalties of 10 percent on a book that retails for $20, the book must sell five thousand copies before she is entitled to begin collecting royalties.

It seems likely that a similar trend may emerge in the computer software industry. Thousands of individual software developers create products and technologies on their own, in their garages and basements, and then try to sell this software to software publishers for fixed fees and/or royalty payments. The same is true of digital content developers. There are many opportunities for creators to develop content on spec and sell it after the fact, as opposed to creating it as a salaried employee. This is very similar to the film industry in Hollywood, where thousands of film scripts are written each year on spec and then attempts are made to sell them.

Generally, new media entrepreneurs act on their ideas quickly, make their mark and money, then sell them off and start all over again. If you're starting a new media project, you might want to look towards the future and consider who might buy you out. (Maybe a little too optimistic, but why not!) A tip in these circumstances: keep careful track of any IP rights you've acquired or licensed along the way, as any potential purchaser of your new media product will want to see proof of ownership of IP prior to investing any money in your project.

Employees and New Media Entrepreneurs

Whether you're retraining or acquiring new skills, there are two options for applying them: you may attract an employer or you may decide to work for yourself. Nothing new here. However, there is some novelty in these two types of work situations, regarding the shift in the amount of people in each category (and the growth in the self-employed category). Let's look at each category. What it means to be an employee is obvious: someone hires us, we get paid, deductions are at source, and we get benefits like dental plans. Let's look at the other category: nonemployees includes everyone from freelance writers and designers to SOHOs (small office home office) to cottage industries to entrepreneurs. But in the digital age, many who are not working for someone else are "IP entrepreneurs" or "new media entrepreneurs." And in this era, more and more of us will be IP entrepreneurs because it's fun. Plus it's a way to make a living. And often a way to make a living which allows us to control our own time.

Tips for New Media Entrepreneurs

If you're looking for new media opportunities, keep in mind that the possibilities on the Web are probably underexplored, and we are only in the beginning stages. If you're creative, innovative, and move fast, you'll be getting in on the ground floor. Plus, the start-up and operating costs, thanks to the Internet, may be significantly lower than those associated with other new businesses.

When exploring digital opportunities, keep in mind that much of what is digitized is "old" or existing content. In many situations, we are buying and selling the same content we've previously bought and sold. How many of us gave away our vinyl recordings and replaced them with CDs? Will we once again replace them with DVDs? The sound-recording business is notorious for reselling the same content (back catalogs), as record companies continue to make money on true and tested music. Perhaps the same can be said of Hollywood remaking classic films and adapting books into screenplays and films. The interesting thing is that most people probably cannot tell the difference in the sound quality of newer recordings — many of us replaced our vinyl because of convenience and not necessarily for better sound quality. People generally buy the same things again and again — a fact that new media entrepreneurs might keep in mind.

Sometimes content you currently own — a collection of print articles or collection of photographs — can be repackaged, or moved to a different platform, from print to CD-ROM, from a Web site to a touch-screen kiosk. Consider other markets, and other audiences (e.g., translations). You could digitize nondigital works so that people can then easily copy, search, manipulate, and transmit it.

The DVD (digital versatile disc) is an exciting new development which could transform the digital property industry as DVD starts to replace CD-ROM. A DVD holds 4.7 gigabytes of data, approximately equal to seven CD-ROM platters, and is an excellent medium for mapping programs and databases which can span several CD-ROMs. Also, DVD has capacity for a large quantity of video (over two hours of full-motion video with excellent quality video and audio). Further, DVDs play on both televisions and computers.

Technology provides us with more choices, and the consumer is now used to an abundance of choice, whether it's picking the ending to a story on a CD-ROM or being able to access content in more than one medium. This is the consumer to whom we must cater. In general, people are seeking variety, customization, interactivity, quality content, and speed of access.

A further point to keep in mind is that the dividing line between the content provider and the distributor or deliverer of that content is not always distinct on the Net. Larger companies like Microsoft develop their own content as well as distribute it. A new media entrepreneur might develop content and license it to an online service for distribution purposes, or she might choose to distribute her content on her own Web site. In developing your own new media entrepreneurial ventures, keep in mind that the Web can offer you instantaneous distribution to a worldwide audience at a minimal cost.

One thing to keep in mind is that you may not need the "ultimate" product in order to make a profit. Rather, a product that is needed by a large quantity of people may lead you to that grand profit. For instance, the two most valuable patents over the last fifty years have been tranquilizers and anti-ulcerants, notwithstanding the fact that they are not even the most important drugs developed during this time. Their value lies in the fact that these pills are useful to billions of people around the world at some point in their lives since we almost all suffer from over-anxiety or indigestion at some time. Thus, their value lies in their usefulness to a huge market.

Digital Examples

Television? The word is half Latin and half Greek. No good can come of it.

— attributed to C.P. Scott (1846–1932) of the *Manchester Guardian*[4]

Below are several examples of opportunities for earning income in an information-obsessed society. Some are opportunities for employees and some for new media entrepreneurs. Some are specific and require a linear route to reach them, while others are ideas and will require some creativity in making them a reality. And, of course, some are based on projections about where the economy is going and how information will be accessible and valuable to individuals and organizations in the future. In addition, as we witness the growth of electronic commerce and online transactions, we will likely see a large increase in the amount of products and services for sale on the Internet.

Lastly, you might want to return to chapter 2 to review the kinds of natural resources and digital assets owned by yourself and others, as this may start you thinking about the types of projects, works, and ventures you might pursue.

Visual Artists

Art on the Internet isn't threatening. Go when you feel like it. Stay as long as you want.

— Janine Cirincione, former director of the Jack Tilton Gallery in New York and now the producer of art content for the Microsoft Network

A recent newspaper article highlighted the career of a photographer who began by shooting door-to-door baby pictures and now earns $1 million in annual revenue, with plans to reach $20 million in three to five years. Simply put, this photographer's company digitizes corporate records, including advertising, annual reports, videos, trade show presentations, employee newsletters, and Internet and intranet images. Once digitized, these images can be used again and again by the corporation.

To obtain her expertise, the photographer began by providing potential clients with two digitized reports for free, to help her develop experience in this area. She also spent two years perfecting her own talents and skills on the computer to ensure the digital images on which she worked maintained a professional quality. Her own words can perhaps serve as a motto for us all:

> *We're translators. We're bringing things from the old format into the new. . . . We're not throwing out the past. We're making the past comfortable in the present.*[5]

Joseph Squier, an artist whose Web site The Place (*http://gertrude. art.uiuc.edu/ludgate/the/place.html*) is considered a "classic," likes the direct sale model. He thinks we should look at artists as content providers rather than as object producers. He compares this to the music business where no one confuses a live concert with the purchase of a recorded CD.

Digitized images have a huge market in various industries and for various purposes, including advertising, promotions, and editorial. They can be licensed for use in presentations and reports, brochures, advertisements and promotions, packaging, books, newsletters, and magazines. They can also be used on T-shirts and other clothing items, mugs, book jackets, greeting cards, postcards, and posters.

Digitizing the Nondigital

PictureVision Inc. (*http://www.picturevision.com/*) has developed a consumer-oriented system to deal with your family photos, as well as any other photos. By checking the "PhotoNet" box on the film envelope (and paying the additional fee) when you go to get your photos developed at participating retailers, you are assigned a film identification (ID) number or access code with instructions on how to view your photos online. Your photos remain online for thirty days, during which time you can share them at no extra cost with family and friends around the world by sending them the film ID or emailing the images to them. (Believe me, this is fun.) You can also download the photos to your computer, print them, edit them, or post them on Web pages. And for a fee, you can order reprints and enlargements and have them mailed to you or to someone else. As of May 1997, the company claims to deal with 150,000 rolls of film a month.

Filling Those Web Sites

We're all watching the development of the Web from "rehashed" content to grand new designs and packaged interactive and dynamic information as we enter the second generation of Web sites. Web site designers are now calling themselves "information architects" and "interface designers." For people who enjoy reading about the beginnings of Hollywood and what it was like to be writing the scripts for the studios back then, today's digital medium may be equally as exciting. Creators and new media entrepreneurs live in exciting times. Whenever I read an article that says the Internet is overrated, I just shake my head and think, no, it's underrated. It just hasn't found its niche yet.

One way for the Web to find its niche is to improve the content, whether it's the quality of the actual content or the presentation of it. And with corporate America now behind it, its speed has just accelerated. Although people are still looking towards innovative teenagers or retraining current employees to get them on the Web, they are also willing to pay top bucks for professionals, whether it's to write computer code, create hypertext links, scan images, manipulate digital files of graphics and text, or actually create original content. The demand for professional Web site designers and new media content creators has already exceeded the supply. And to fill that demand we are seeing high-quality magazine designers like Roger Black turning to a digital career. In the past, Black has worked for *Newsweek*, *Premiere*, the *San Francisco Examiner*, and the *New York Times*. Of course, there seems to be money to be made in Web sites and creating an Internet presence. Larger companies are now spending several hundred thousand dollars to design Web sites, and in companies that have many divisions, the expenditures can be multiplied.

Black's Web site for the Discovery Network cost more than $1 million, and a staff of ten Web designers regularly updates the site (presumably for a handsome fee).[6]

Movie Studios

For those of you who have been on the Web for more than two years, you will have noticed that Hollywood movie studio Web sites initially contained the press kit for a movie, photographs, plot synopses, and actors' biographies. Pretty boring! They are now starting to offer more interesting information, as well as links to other Web sites, quizzes, contests, etc. By observing the increase in the quality of content in movie Web sites, it seems that movie studios are very interested in posting valuable content. And from what I hear and see (unofficially, of course), the studios are hiring people to help develop that valuable content, in part due to one of the underlying principles in Hollywood — they don't want their competitors to get a lead on them. Of course, if the major movie studios are concerned with quality content, this will filter down to all of the movie companies, and probably to other sorts of media and nonmedia companies, thereby providing opportunities for a variety of content creators.

Digital Publishers

> *Some of us are becoming the men we wanted to marry.*
> — Gloria Steinem

We often hear that the Internet has made everyone a publisher. As a new media entrepreneur, you should think about all the varied and wonderful publishing opportunities on the Internet. Much of the publishing we see on the Internet is not for profit. For instance, many e-zines on the Web are available for free to the general public around the world. But this is changing as people begin to understand the value of well-packaged information. Money is being exchanged for that packaged information.

Publishing on the Net is not, however, limited to a Web site or e-zine. Another way to publish is to have your own listserv, which allows you to "push" information to your readers via email as opposed to having them go to your Web site to access it. With the touch of a button on your computer keyboard, you can electronically send packaged information instantaneously to an unlimited number of people around the world. Although many listservs are free, there's no reason why subscribers would not pay for the right kind of packaged information, or why advertisers would not cover your costs and allow you to earn some revenue. For example, you could start a listserv on opportunities for new media entrepreneurs which could send announcements once a week for a yearly fee of $10.

Archives

Packaging information in a way that makes it easily accessible to consumers is very important in this time of information overload. Archiving radio shows or print magazines for their initial audience and for new audiences can prove to be valuable resources of revenue for the new media entrepreneur.

Databases

> *The greatest thing since they reinvented unsliced bread.*
> — William Keegan, *Observer*

There have always been databases around homes and offices, even though not officially named as such. Recently, databases are being recognized as extremely valuable assets, not only for one's own purposes, but also for the purposes of being licensed (rented) or sold to others.

What exactly is a database? It can be as simple as your personal telephone book, the guest list from your wedding, or a collection of your vacation photographs. At the office, it could be a list of your customers, a list of customers that drink tea rather than coffee, an inventory of consultants in a certain area, or a catalog of your products. In generic terms, a database is a collection of information. That information can be on paper or stored electronically on your computer. For our purposes, it is a collection of valuable information that you should consider a business asset. And keep in mind that the collected data need not be merely text but can include photographs, illustrations, logos, sound, and video.

In 1995 in the United States, online information distribution by databases generated total annual revenue of US$11.1 billion.

If you're a history buff, you might already have created your own database about the best books to read about World War II. In fact, you may have started this "hobby" database twenty years ago when you were in high school — perhaps it's now twenty or a hundred pages long — and it might have some value out there! Keep in mind that the founders of Apple Computers started out as hobbyists!

Combos

How about a combination of different kinds of publishing? I recently began a print newsletter (*http://copyrightlaws.com*) to be published three times a year. For the cost of subscribing to the print newsletter, subscribers additionally benefit from email and Web publications. A subscription includes:

➡ three comprehensive print newsletters a year

➡ a free email subscription to the online newsletter *Copyright and New Media Legal News*, with back issues archived at the National Library of Canada (*http://collection.nlc-bnc.ca/100 /201/300/copyright-a/index.html*)

➡ free email alerts containing important capsuled news events, sent between issues of the print version (via a listserv)

And you might be interested in knowing that the great majority of advertising for subscribers is done online through listservs, that all articles are submitted, edited, and returned to contributor via email, and that all copy goes to the designer via email.

Since the VCR did not replace going to the movies, nor television replace radio, nor radio replace the printed book, chances are that electronic media are not going to replace all other media. This means that if you're in the content-providing business, you need to be concerned about all media, even though your main focus may be digital media. In fact, the media feed off one another. I often find references to books when surfing the Web, then go to the bookstore to purchase the book. Similarly, you might read a movie review then go see the movie, or you might see a movie, then order its soundtrack from a Web site.

Digitizing Public Domain Works

Works *not* protected by copyright can be great underlying resources for your digitization projects. For instance, U.S. federal government documents are not protected by copyright. Music of Mozart and works of Shakespeare are in the public domain. Many new media entrepreneurs are discovering this wealth of material for which they do not have to pay. One caution in all of this is that you must use the original work, and not someone else's adapted or value-added version of it.

Sound Recording Producers

So maybe you've always wanted your own record label. This may be your chance. When it comes to music and the Internet, you've probably thought more about purchasing music from Sony and other big-name producers than being your own producer and distributor. But there's computer software out there that allows you to start your very own independent (indie) label, to record barbershop quartets or garage rock bands and make it available to others for purchase.

Now, if you're tone deaf like me, creating your own record label will be of no interest to you. However, you may have noticed how popular audio books are now — from fiction to business books to self-help. As a new media entrepreneur, you might include helpful audio clips on your Web site. In fact, you might even set up an online course to instruct people about a certain subject matter which you enhance with audio recordings that can be listened to in a car.

Broadcasters

The Internet now allows for broadcasts of audio and audiovisual works. This is another opportunity for creators and new media entrepreneurs to have their works distributed through one of the existing online broadcasters, or to produce their own broadcasts of interviews, literary readings, film clips, and so on through their own Web sites.

Educators

The Internet has opened up a whole new realm of education, of all kinds and at all levels. Children living in remote areas can learn from home, as can disabled persons. Business people no longer have to leave their desks to get the latest update in their fields. Parents can be in school while at home with their children. In terms of IP, this means that courses and learning materials will have to be developed that are effective for Internet classrooms and teaching. Scanning a textbook into a computer for distribution over the Internet is not effective. New interactive materials will have to be developed, while existing print materials and textbooks will have to be enhanced and customized. There will be many opportunities for those who understand the new media and have some background in education.

Legal and Quasi-Legal Positions

The new digital economy presents many different opportunities for an IP lawyer, including computer and Internet law, art and entertainment law, patent, trademark, and copyright law, or a combination of any of those.

Rights clearances is a rapidly growing field with respect to new media. Because a single CD-ROM can store over 650 megabytes of information, roughly equivalent to 250,000 pages of text, clearing rights can in some cases be a full-time job for someone. Although many may think this is the role of an attorney, in fact, an attorney may hire a nonlawyer to clear rights on his behalf, as it would be less expensive. Book publishers have rights departments and film companies have staff to deal with clearing the rights of underlying works. With projects like the Microsoft *Encarta* multimedia encyclopedia requiring over 6,000 individual rights clearances, this is definitely a growing area.

Agents

Just as agents represent print book and script writers, actors, and others, agents are now also representing content owners, especially in Hollywood where the use of agents is the standard in the industry, as opposed to creators representing themselves. Anyone interested in pursuing an agent role in the new media industry should be aware that this industry attracts many self-starters who often represent themselves and their products, and so the creators themselves may be your competition as an agent.

Other Opportunities

> ### *Being a specialist is one thing, getting a job is another.*
> — Stephen Leacock, *The Boy I Left behind Me*

The list of new media opportunities is "virtually" limitless, and new opportunities are constantly arising. As with any new enterprise, you should know your market, do your research, check out the competition, and feel passionately about your product or service. Use the many search engines, including Yahoo! (*http://*

www.yahoo.com/), Lycos (*http://www.lycos.com/*), Excite (*http://www.
excite.com/*), AltaVista (*http://www.altavista.digital.com/*) and others,
to find businesses similar to your own. Understand the Internet
population by looking at various statistics and information about
online use and the demographics of Net users — O'Reilly and
Associates (*http://www.ora.com/*), the Software Publishers Association (*http://www.spa.org/*), International Data Corporation (*http://
www.idcresearch.com/*), and Forrester Research Inc. (*http://www.
forrester.com/*) are just a few of the available information sources.
Select the digital property that you know will bring a profit on
the Internet. And if at first you don't succeed, modify your idea
and try again. When you stake your claim in cyberspace, remember that the Internet is a "live" market, and often requires that
you continuously adapt your products and services to meet market demands.

Libraries and Museums

Libraries and museums around the world have a huge amount
of natural resources, whether protected by copyright law or not,
which can be digitized and used in many different manners,
including those that may not yet exist. The press has covered Bill
Gates's activities in this arena. Since at least the early 90s, he has
been acquiring the electronic rights to thousands of images,
including the well-known Bettmann photo archives, purchased
in October 1995. His company Corbis (*http://www.corbis.com/*) is
responsible for this part of his business, and although they have
been active in obtaining e-rights, Corbis has not gone to press
with hundreds of CD-ROMs. Rather, Corbis has been focusing on
building its library of digitally stored images that have value for
CD-ROMs and the Internet, and that will increasingly interest
corporations and individuals over the next several years.

Even before Corbis bought Bettmann, it already had e-rights to
500,000 images from such renowned places as the National
Gallery of London, the Philadelphia Museum, and the Barnes
Foundation, as well as from photographers like Roger Ressmeyer
and Galen Rowell. And that was in 1995! The Bettmann Archive

(founded by Otto L. Bettmann) has approximately 16 million images. Although it includes medical and technical drawings, the archive is principally comprised of 11.5 million photographs, ranging from Marilyn Monroe to Malcolm X, from Depression mothers to the Duchess of Windsor.

What are others doing with their libraries of IP? At Viacom, each sector of the company is digitizing IP at its own pace. This includes the publishing, movie, and music businesses which encompass Simon and Schuster, Paramount, and MTV. The speed is basically being determined by the value of the digitized material — what sells gets converted more quickly. A simple rule to follow!

Investing in IP

The information in this chapter may provide you with some idea of the types of companies, where they are public ones, in which you might invest. If you are going to invest in hardware companies, invest in ones that also produce software, because hardware is useless without software — and content is what's going to fill the Internet.

Although many people would rather invest in countries where IP protection is strong, you might also consider investing in companies in Third World countries — in Latin America, for instance — where the pressure is quickly increasing to provide greater IP protection.

Final Word

Now that you have some of the tools necessary to market your digital property, whether through traditional or digital means, imagine a world in which every computer is a newsstand, bookstore, art gallery, museum, radio, television, and movie theater. This is the world in which we now exist. And you own a computer and you own content, so why not market that content and share it with others? Start now by anticipating the changes to come and by adapting your knowledge and skills in order to succeed in the digital economy.

Everyone is searching for a way to make a buck on the Internet. The best advice is to get out there, now, while there is still a shortage of people who are knowledgeable about IP and a growing number of positions in IP. It's possible that there is a small window to succeed, so why not be the leader of the revolution! Get out there, be innovative, take a risk, and have some fun.

End Notes

1. Ann Okerson, "Who Owns Digital Works," *Scientific American*, July 1996, p. 80.

2. Seth Schiesel, "Payoff Still Elusive in Internet Gold Rush," *New York Times*, 2 January 1997, p C17.

3. For their story, see Laurence A. Canter and Martha S. Siegel, *How to Make a Fortune on the Information Highway* (New York: HarperCollins, 1994).

4. C.P. Scott, quoted in Asa Briggs, *The BBC: The First Fifty Years* (Toronto: Oxford University Press, 1985), p. 239.

5. Mary Fote (president of Medea Group), quoted in Janet McFarland, "Photographer Takes Shot at Multimedia," *Globe and Mail*, 2 December 1996, p. B7.

6. And these are 1995 figures. See Glenn Rifkin, "Increasingly, Top Designers Are Drawn to the Web," *New York Times*, 27 November 1995, p. D7.

.

PART 4

Protecting Your Property

CHAPTER 8

Stealing Nothing:
Piracy of Digital Property

The United States took on China over pirating intellectual property for the first time in 1903, when trademarked foreign products first flowed out of Chinese factories. The Chinese figured that if they signed an agreement and ignored it, Washington would soon forget about the whole thing. They were right.

Ninety-two years later, China's leaders signed another accord, this time promising to keep their hands off Winnie-the-Pooh videotapes and Windows 95 CD-ROMs.

— David E. Sanger, *New York Times*[1]

One of the major reasons why some content holders are holding back or hesitant to distribute their IP on the Internet is that it's so easy, quick, and inexpensive for that IP to be stolen from the Net.

Change in Attitude

"Everything is funny as long as it is happening to somebody else," Will Rogers once said, but little did he know that someone like me would apply his words to the Internet. In fact, Will Rogers's words may capture the essence of why, despite certain contrary opinions on this topic, the notion of protecting IP will *not* disappear in the twenty-first century. In fact, IP will grow and be as valuable and as omnipresent as tangible property. And with that growth, it seems logical that the unauthorized or pirated use of IP will not be as prevalent as it currently is and may even decrease.

One of the reasons why piracy will probably decline is that it might have been "funny" to steal IP when it belonged mostly to megacorporations like IBM and Microsoft (that is, in the form of stealing computer software), but it is quickly losing its humor as it becomes equivalent to stealing your neighbor's bicycle — and that's what's happening or is about to happen in your neighborhood. As we realize that IP relates to what we all do and create every day, whether at home or work, we are more likely to guard our own property, and as a result, we are likely to be more respectful of IP that belongs to other people.

What's Happening in Your Neighborhood

Recently, a friend offered to lend me his newly acquired copy of WordPerfect to install on my computer. When I replied that I couldn't borrow it from him, he asked why not, explaining that the software can be copied more than once. "It can be," I replied, "but not legally."

Not long ago, I was in one of my favorite pubs in Toronto celebrating a friend's birthday, only half listening to her while eavesdropping on the conversation taking place on the bar stools behind me. I heard the man say that his company doesn't distribute software in China because once one copy is in the country, the software is illegally reproduced and distributed like wildfire.

These two anecdotes separately and together expose the roots of piracy of IP. First, the general public does not consistently understand what constitutes piracy, and second, it is extremely easy, fast, and inexpensive to copy and distribute pirated goods. And I'll add a third point: it seems that even those who do understand that pirating IP is illegal will still do so (much like jaywalking or speeding in one's automobile).

Insight Canada Research for the Canadian Coalition against Insurance Fraud recently asked 1,600 Canadians the following two questions: (1) what would you do if you put seventy-five cents in a newspaper box and a passerby asked if he could take a second (unpaid for) newspaper while the box was open, and (2) what would you do if you paid $300 for accounting software and an acquaintance asked if he could copy the disks. The results: 12 percent would allow the passerby to steal the seventy-five-cent newspaper, but 52 percent would assist in the theft of the $300 computer software.[2]

Now where does this leave the creator or the new media entrepreneur?

History Repeats Itself

> *Reproducing intellectual property without permission from its owner amounts to theft.*
> — Margaret Atwood

Theft of IP is not a new issue. Rather, it is one which has gained significance with the advent of each new technology. This has been true ever since Gutenberg invented the printing press, and the control of unauthorized uses of IP has become extremely difficult with newer technologies like the photocopying machine, scanners, and now the Internet. Some people predict that the protection of IP is not possible or practical on the Net. If this is correct, then what will happen to those who create IP? If these creators are not compensated for the use of their works while others profit from those works, will creators continue to create new works?

The issue broadens as the Internet allows just about everyone to be a creator of IP (even if it's only by email communication), as well as a publisher and distributor of IP. Copyright laws around the world protect the way we express our ideas (though not the ideas themselves) in words, images, video, and music, but legal protection even with civil and criminal sanctions does not seem to be a sufficient deterrent to prevent unauthorized uses of IP. In most cases, copyright statutes in various countries provide adequate remedies for copyright infringement. What we're missing is the "teeth," the knowledge, the means (the money), and the expedited ways to enforce our rights and remedies. Unfortunately, technology makes the piracy of IP too easy and, in many instances, makes the enforcement of our rights not worth the effort or the heavy expense.

What Is Piracy?

Pirates issued their own Chinese version of the Encyclopaedia Britannica in Taiwan before the legitimate edition could be published, kept selling it despite court rulings and, with amazing chutzpah, warned consumers to "watch out for fakes."

— Gary M. Hoffman and George T. Marcou, *Washington Post*[3]

Before delving further into this topic, we should all understand the meaning of piracy. It is the unauthorized use or illicit duplication of legitimate materials protected by copyright law. An example of piracy is making a compilation of songs copied from various CDs. Print books, computer software, and CD-ROMs may be pirated versions, and music CDs copied onto tape may also be pirated versions. Piracy is a violation or infringement (a term used in copyright statutes) of copyright and may refer to "stealing" protected works from the Internet.

Copyright law may be infringed directly, by using one of the exclusive rights of the copyright holder without permission, or indirectly through a commercial activity involving a copyright-protected work. Moral rights can be violated through any act or omission which is contrary to any of the moral rights of the creator. In addition, unauthorized recordings of performances and uses of such recordings may be a violation of the law in certain countries. According to the European Report of the European Commission (1991), "Some 500,000 pages are photocopied every minute throughout the world, and this phenomenon is growing every day thanks to the possibilities offered by new reproduction technology. . . . that is 260 billion pages per year."[4]

There are a number of terms used in connection with copyright infringement or related activities. Some of these terms are set out below.

Plagiarism

Plagiarism is a term often used in association with literary works like books. According to *Black's Law Dictionary*, plagiarism is "the act of appropriating the literary composition of another, or parts or passages of his writings, or the ideas or language of the same, and passing them off as the product of one's own mind." As such, plagiarism may violate the right to reproduce a copyright-protected work and may also violate the moral right of the author to have her name associated with her work. Where plagiarism is an appropriation of ideas, without the appropriation of the actual expression of those ideas, it is not a violation of copyright since copyright does not protect ideas.

> *When you steal from one author, it's plagiarism; if you steal from many, it's research.*
> — William Mizner

Note that the above quote is not a legal opinion!

Bootlegging

Bootlegging includes the unauthorized recording of a live event, such as a concert. Bring your tape recorder to a concert and you too can make a bootleg tape (though I don't recommend it!).

Counterfeiting

Counterfeiting is making a copy of something without authority and deceiving or defrauding the public by passing that copy off as original or genuine. Where you have a counterfeit product, such as a music cassette or computer software, that item as well as any affixed labels and packaging are illegally reproduced.

Hackers

The terms *hacker* and *cracker* are used to refer to a person who "breaks and enters" into a computer system via a modem or other computer communications device, usually to steal data, sabotage information, or merely look around at information that is intended as private. Also, hackers may infringe copyright laws by illegally copying and distributing computer software, or cause some mischief or damage to data, and be involved with other computer-related crimes.

Softlifting

> *Computer software is the only industry in the world that empowers every customer to become a manufacturing subsidiary.*
>
> — Ken Wasch, president of the Software Publishers Association

The computer software industry uses the term *softlifting* to refer to the making of extra copies of software for use within an organization or at home. For example, a company might purchase one copy of a computer program and then use it on four different computers within the organization. Swapping computer disks and programs with colleagues and friends also falls within this category and is the most common type of computer software piracy.

Rentals

Certain rentals without the authorization of the copyright owner are illegal. For instance, a store renting copyable computer software may fall into this category.

Internet/Email/BBS Piracy

This would cover the unauthorized copying or scanning of IP like text, images, and computer software into a computer and transmitting them over the Internet or via a bulletin board system (BBS). Certain acts (primarily commercial ones) of downloading and printing from the Internet may also constitute an infringement of copyright. Further, reproducing text, images, music, and film clips for purposes of sending them to one or many persons via email may be illegal.

Moral Rights Infringement

In all of the different types of infringement, the copy may be an inferior reproduction of the original work, resulting, for example, in poor sound quality in the case of a sound recording, in poor picture quality in the case of an audio-video recording, or containing bugs in the case of computer software, which arguably are violations of moral rights because they harm the reputation of the creator. So in any claim of alleged infringement, moral rights infringement would probably also be claimed (provided moral rights are protected in that country's copyright statutes where the piracy claim is made).

Signs of Pirated Works

Identifying pirated works can be as simple as spotting a photocopied label on a video or computer software disk, or inferior packaging. Another sign is the quality of the work — is the software problematic or does it contain a virus? Or is the viewing and/or sound quality of a videotape not up to par? Another less obvious sign is works being sold at greatly reduced prices. Further, in certain industries like the computer software industry, works must be sold by authorized dealers; unauthorized dealers, including street vendors, may be selling pirated items.

If you are concerned that your own works are being used without your permission, you should consult a copyright lawyer as soon as possible. If you come across other people's works that you suspect are pirated, there are hotlines in many countries for reporting pirated computer software, sound recordings, and videos (see appendix C). As well, your local police may be of assistance.

Piracy in the Digital World

Unfortunately there is one thing standing between me and that property — the rightful owners.

— Harvey Korman, in *Blazing Saddles* (written by Andrew Bergman, Mel Brooks, Richard Pryor, Norman Steinberg, and Alan Under)

Although all copyright works are susceptible to being copied without permission, and the rights of the copyright owner thereby infringed, digital property is particularly susceptible to illegal copying. There are a number of reasons for this: copying often takes place at home, because the activity is private and because more people have computers at home than photocopiers or printing presses; copying is easy, inexpensive, and fast; and the quality of the copy is often identical to the original. In many ways, the Internet has made IP more susceptible to piracy.

Further, many people on the Internet mistakenly believe that anything on it can be freely copied and distributed without obtaining permission. Although there is some discussion of "implied" permission (permission through the behavior of actually posting a work on the Net), we see more and more IP owners placing copyright notices and warnings on their Web sites. In general, these notices say something to the effect that all works on the Web site are protected by copyright. They may provide the Web surfer with permission to use the works in certain circumstances indicating private, personal, and noncommercial uses, but usually prohibit further uses without permission from the copyright holder.

Other IP owners have gone further by instituting lawsuits to stop the unauthorized use of their works and by sending what are called demand letters, requesting that all copyright-infringing materials be removed from the particular Web site. The Presley estate, for example, complained about the violation of its rights to the owner of an Elvis Presley Web site, who then removed the infringing IP materials.

Some Recent Lawsuits

A variety of lawsuits in relation to new media have been instituted in the past few years. Below is a summary of selected cases to show what's happening out there.

Internet Suits

On July 23, 1996, a civil copyright infringement lawsuit against Seattle-based Max Butler was filed in the U.S. District Court in Seattle, alleging that Butler illegally uploaded copyright-protected software to a file transfer protocol (FTP) site operated by an Internet service provider (ISP), for distribution across the Internet. The Software Publishers Association (SPA) filed this suit on behalf of its members, stating that SPA could have sued the ISP for copyright infringement but chose not to in this case because of this ISP's immediate proactive remedial action. In October 1996, SPA initiated legal action against a different ISP, GeoCities, after being informed that many people using GeoCities were allegedly making illegal content available. In November 1996, the lawsuit was settled out of court. GeoCities removed the infringing content and is ensuring that copyright infringement will not occur on, or through, its servers.

Online Services

One hundred and forty music publishers sued the online service CompuServe, alleging that its subscribers had uploaded and downloaded more than five hundred music compositions. CompuServe agreed to pay US$500,000 in damages and to cooperate with music publishers to help them license their works to online users.[5]

BBS Suits

In the first case in Canada of its kind, the operator of a Montreal-area bulletin board system (BBS) known as 90 North was indicted under Canadian law in August 1994 for the illegal distribution of multiple copies of unlicensed software published by Lotus, Microsoft, Novell, and Novell/WordPerfect Applications Group. The investigation was conducted through a series of undercover subscriptions to the BBS and a subsequent trap by the Royal Canadian Mounted Police (RCMP). The board's operator pleaded guilty and was fined Can$20,000.

In a highly publicized case, a BBS operator in the United States was held liable when his users posted scanned copies from *Playboy* magazine, even though he claimed he was not aware of his subscribers' copying.[6]

Electronic Rights Owners Band Together

On October 16, 1996, Belgian journalists won a major e-rights victory in the Tribunal de Première Instance de Bruxelles. The Professional Journalists Association of Belgium, the Journalists Copyright Society, the Multi-media Society of Visual Arts and Authors, and some twenty individual journalists initiated an action against SCRI Central Station, a database that put journalists' work online, on the Internet, without permission and was also violating their moral rights. Created in July 1995, Central

Station is owned by a group of eleven major Belgian publishers of the daily and weekly press. The judge found that Central Station committed violations of copyright by transmitting the articles online without the permission of the writers and often without giving the writers their due credit. The judge ordered the immediate cessation of all such transmissions as well as a series of fines to be paid to the plaintiffs.

In a U.S. suit filed in December 1993 by a group of National Writers' Union (*http://www.nwu.org/nwu/*) members against the *New York Times* et al., led by NWU president Jonathan Tasini, the court was asked to determine whether publishers may place the contents of their periodicals into electronic databases and onto CD-ROMs without first obtaining the permission of the freelance writers whose contributions are included in those periodicals. The freelance journalists claimed that without first securing permission, this would infringe the copyright that each writer holds in his or her individual articles. The defendant publishers and electronic service providers argued that they have not improperly used the journalists' individual contributions, and have permission to reproduce the articles in the electronic database and CD-ROM versions of the newspapers and magazines in which those articles first appeared. On August 13, 1997, the court ruled in favor of the defendants. A copy of the decision is published by the *New York Law Journal* (*http://www.nylj.com/links/tasini.html*). This is a contentious decision from the plaintiff's perspective, and further court proceedings may deal with it.

Similarly, in Ontario, a class action lawsuit was commenced on September 10, 1996, by writer Heather Robertson against the Thomson Corporation and its affiliates, including the California-based Information Access Company (IAC), on behalf of all creators of original literary or artistic works published in print media in Canada who own the e-rights to their works and whose works allegedly have been or are being infringed by the defendants through inclusion in electronic media. Toronto-based Thomson is the owner of the *Globe and Mail* (Canada's national newspaper) and many other media properties. IAC supplies commercial full-text magazine and newspaper article databases via Nexis, Compu-Serve, Dow Jones News Retrieval, Dialog, and many restricted online libraries. The plaintiff seeks Can$100 million in damages.

A Successful Negotiation

In June 1996, Norwegian newspaper journalists came to an agreement with newspapers in that country concerning payment for the republication of their articles in an electronic format. Newspapers often take the position that they can republish mate-rials electronically — on the Internet or in a database, for exam-ple — without paying journalists a fee above that paid for the print version. The Norwegian contract acknowledges that trans-mitting stories or pictures online constitutes a second publica-tion, and newspapers have agreed to pay the equivalent of US$150 a year for using a reporter's material on the Internet and US$75 for use in databases available to the public.

Similar types of negotiations are happening in various other jurisdictions, though often the parties are finding it difficult to agree on terms.

The Dangerous Side of Digital Copying

Digital copying may be more harmful than other illicit copying because distribution is so simple. Unlike trying to distribute a photocopied book or bootleg video, digital works can easily be distributed around the world, usually instantaneously. The com-puter software industry, one of the oldest digital-based indus-tries, has since its inception been faced by the problems inherent to digital technology.

A study released in May 1997 by the Software Publishers Associ-ation (*http://www.spa.org/*) and the Business Software Alliance (*http://www.bsa.org/*), both trade associations that represent com-puter software publishers and fight piracy in the computer soft-ware industries, estimated that US$11.2 billion was lost in 1996 due to computer software piracy. The study estimates that of the

523 million new copies of business software applications used around the world in 1996, 225 million units (more than 40%) were pirated. The region with the highest overall piracy rate was Eastern Europe (80%), and countries with high rates included Vietnam (99%), China (96%), Oman (95%), and Russia (91%). By contrast, lower software piracy rates were evident in North America (28%), the United Kingdom (34%), Australia (32%), Denmark (35%), New Zealand (35%), and Germany (36%).

The sound recording industry has also experienced high piracy rates. According to the International Federation of the Phono-graphic Industry (IFPI), estimated sales of pirated prerecorded music in 1995 were US$2.1 billion worldwide. This means that there were unauthorized sales of 955 million units, consisting of 866 million cassettes, 85 million CDs, and 4 million LPs. According to these statistics, one in every five sound recordings is an illegal copy. Russia is the largest pirate market, with illegal sales of 222 million units valued at US$363 million and accounting for 62 percent of sales in the country. Next is the United States at $279.4 million, followed by China at US$168 million, Italy at US$145.6 million, Brazil at US$118.8 million, Germany at US$92.2 million, Mexico at US$85.3 million, India at US$82.1 million, Pakistan at US$62.1 million, and France at US$58.5 million.

Books, videos, and many other works are also being pirated around the world in large quantities and causing many copyright holders to lose sales and revenue.

Who's Liable?

Digital piracy brings with it new issues. In the nondigital world, if someone photocopies your print book without permission, it's fairly clear that the person photocopying your book is the one who is infringing your rights. However, things are not so clear with respect to uses of digital works, especially on the Internet. The question here is, When your work appears on the Internet without your permission, whom do you sue — the Internet provider, Web site owner, telephone company, or the person/ company who posted your work to the Internet? Unfortunately, there is no clear answer at this time. It will be up to future legislation and/or court cases to help clarify this issue. In fact, the court cases mentioned above are among those that have already begun to deal with this issue.[7]

Precautions to Take

Whereas piracy was once generally aimed at larger companies in commercial industries like software, publishing, film, and sound recording, it is now proliferating in all sectors of the marketplace. If you are the creator or owner of IP, there's a strong possibility your rights will be infringed at some point. Practically speaking, you don't want to sue anyone to enforce your rights. Initiating a court action is expensive, energy-draining, and time-consuming. There is a place and need for it, but there are also various steps you can take to help prevent unauthorized uses of your works. For example, it's a good idea to always place a copyright notice on your works, although it is not mandatory in many countries in order to acquire copyright protection. (Copyright notices are discussed in chapter 6.)

Also, make it as easy as possible for consumers to obtain permission to use your work. At the end of the copyright notice you might state something to the effect of the following: "Requests for permission to use these materials, or parts of them, should be addressed to:" and then provide a contact name, mailing address (or snail mail address, as it is now often referred to), telephone and fax numbers, and email address — four ways in which a consumer can reach you to get permission to use your work.

You might also consider joining one of the copyright collectives. I belong (for no fee) to a reprography collective, or what's also called a copyright collective for photocopying. This means that when my work is photocopied in certain educational institutions, libraries, and other organizations, a fee is paid to the collective which in turn is distributed to me and other creators. A couple of years ago, a check was sent to me in the amount of $50 for being a member of the collective. In 1996, the check was more than five times that amount. We are already seeing such collectives emerging for the use of IP in digital media. A list of photocopying collectives around the world is available from the International Federation of Reproduction Rights Organizations (*http://www.kopinor.no/IFRRO/* or *http://www.copyright.com/ifrro/*).

Also, proper licensing of IP, as discussed earlier in chapter 5, will help ensure less piracy.

Monitoring the Use of Your Works

Another major problem in enforcing your rights on the Internet is the difficulty in knowing who is using what. With the vast amount of information on the Net, how do you keep an eye on your work? One of the reasons copyright collectives for photo-copying began was because rights holders could not possibly monitor the use of their works. It didn't matter if the photo-copying was taking place in the same office, down the street, or at the opposite end of the country or world, it was pretty much impossible to keep an eye on it. Even with e-rights collectives, you might want to make a habit of regularly searching the Inter-net (once a month, let's say) for any unauthorized uses of your digital property. Use one of the many powerful search engines to look for your name or certain topics. There are companies (and probably new ones coming aboard all the time) who do this on behalf of their clients.

Enforcing Your Rights

Content owners are generally responsible for the enforcement of their rights. However, there are certain situations where the fed-eral police (such as the FBI or RCMP) may investigate a case of alleged infringement, and the government may take a role in prosecuting the alleged infringers. If you suspect your IP is being used without your permission, it is best to get advice from a copyright lawyer on how to proceed.

Copyright Policies

Because of the increasing awareness of IP, many organizations are concerned about complying with copyright laws and are educating their employees and consultants about the proper use of IP. This is often done in order for these organizations to avoid being sued for illegal activities such as software piracy and illegal photocopying. If you're an IP owner, such policies would certainly benefit you. And if others work for you, you might consider implementing a copyright policy in your own workplace.

Internet Policies

Similarly, many organizations are now instituting Internet policies to deal with copyright issues, like who's responsible when an employee posts unauthorized IP on a company's Web site, as well as with many noncopyright issues, like whether an employee can bind an organization to a contract by virtue of email correspondence or what the ethical and legal considerations are in monitoring employees' email.

Email affords employees the opportunity to infringe another's copyright, misappropriate another's trade secrets or confidential information, or commit the company to a particular position or acceptance of a contract. Although the telephone and fax allow these opportunities, the novelty and ease of use of email and the Internet sometimes result in "sloppy" or unintentional communicating of information. Because that information can be so easily and quickly manipulated, email is potentially more dangerous than other forms of communication. Some people do not realize its potential or recognize the fact that a casual response (in writing of course!) may accidentally and unintentionally lead to a binding agreement, when that same agreement might not have been entered into if done "more formally" through an exchange of snail mail.

Technology to the Rescue

Effective mechanisms for monitoring illegal access, use, reproduction, and manipulation of digital property on the Internet, as well as payment schemes for IP owners, are beginning to set their feet down in cyberspace. There are a number of protection technologies in use and in development which will help owners of digital property to control the use of it. Some of these mechanisms are described below.

➡ **Encryption:** This "hides" the content from an unauthorized user by converting it into code. (Encrypted content can be compared to scrambled satellite signals.) Only someone with the decryption key can recover the original content in a useable form. Encryption helps ensure privacy, as the information is hidden to everyone other than those for whom it is intended.

➡ **Secure containers:** IP is transported in a "secure container" which can be opened with a digital key only when the user agrees to the rules and prices set by the owner of the content. IBM calls their secure container a "Cryptolope" (see *http:// www.databolts.ibm.com/cryptolope.htm*), while Xerox calls their technology "DPRL" or a Digital Property Rights Language. The DPRL encrypts a digital work, such as a book, image, movie, or computer software, and delivers it in a digital envelope with terms and conditions of use.

➡ **Watermarking:** A digital watermark contains data which identifies a work, such as copyright information relating to the name of the copyright owner and date of publication. Watermarks are also used to provide authentication and validation of digital property. This technology allows content owners to track illegal uses and ensure payment. The watermark, which is incorporated into the work itself, can be visible or invisible, and any attempt to remove the data may destroy the work.

There is existing software that allows a copyright owner to create and view a hidden copyright notice. The creator of an image, for example, "watermarks" the image to include his name and an identification number. This is invisible to all others. If the creator of the image suspects an unauthorized version of his image is being used on someone else's Web site, he can download the image to his own computer and read the otherwise invisible identification information to see whether the image is in fact his work that is being used without permission. If the watermark identifies the image as his own, the creator would then have to take the necessary steps against the alleged infringer to enforce his rights.

➡ **Numbering system:** There is an international system of numbering and identifying print books called the International Standard Book Number (ISBN). It is often confused with copyright but is unrelated. The ISBN provides a unique identification number for all books published and is used to facilitate order fulfillment and computer tracking of inventory. Books, pamphlets, educational kits, microforms, microcomputer software, electronic publications, and braille publications have the ISBN. A similar content numbering system may soon become an international standard in the digital world, to provide an easy, efficient way of identifying digital property. For information about the Digital Object Identifier System, see *http://www.doi.org/*.

Final Word

Although attitudes are changing with respect to using IP without permission and technologies are helping to ensure the proper use of IP, the fact remains that digital property is easily stolen, and the crime does not yet seem to carry the same stigma as stealing tangible property. Owners of digital property must take precautions to ensure that their works are used only with their permission and must be aware of the laws and technologies that can help them protect their rights.

End Notes

1. David E. Sanger, "This One Just Might Be a Real Trade War," *New York Times*, 19 May 1996, sec. 4, p. 6.

2. Paul Lina, "Microsoft Files Piracy Lawsuit," *Toronto Star*, 30 May 1997, p. E3.

3. Gary M. Hoffman and George T. Marcou, "Who's Stealing America's Ideas?" *Washington Post*, 5 November 1989, p. C3.

4. Quoted in Tarja Koskinen, "Reprography, Electrocopying, Electronic Delivery and the Exercise of Copyright," paper presented at the WIPO Worldwide Symposium on the Future of Copyright and Neighboring Rights, Paris, June 1994.

5. *Frank Music Corp. v. CompuServe, Inc.* No. 93 Civ. 8153 (S.D.N.Y. 1993).

6. *Playboy Enterprises, Inc. v. George Frena*, 839 F.Supp. 1552 (M.D. FL. 1993).

7. An interesting study that explores the issue of liability for content on the Internet is available on the Canadian Government's Strategis site (*http://strategis.ic.gc.ca/nme/*).

The Tip of the Iceberg

I once asked this literary agent what writing paid the best, and he said, "Ransom notes."

— Gene Hackman, in *Get Shorty* (screenplay by Scott Frank, from the novel by Elmore Leonard)

By now you have a clear understanding of IP and how it is legally protected — but let me set out a couple of cautions before you go on. First, copyright law, which protects your digital property, is complicated and complex. Some people compare copyright law to an onion: the more you understand copyright law, the more layers there are to understand. Alternatively, you can look at copyright law as an iceberg: you now see the tip of the iceberg, but the greater part of it is still under water. Perhaps the best advice here is to be attentive about what you know and don't know. And to keep in mind that copyright law, and the application of it to the Internet, is an evolving area.

Non-IP Rights

The second caution relates to other legal issues of concern to owners of digital property, and which may be confused with copyright law. To illustrate, take a photograph you want to publish in a local magazine or put on your Web site. You're fully aware of copyright implications and are 100 percent sure that you are the rightful, sole, and exclusive owner of the copyright in the photograph. No problem. Wait a minute. In the photograph is a woman standing in front of a tree. *What about her copyright?* Trick question. She doesn't have a copyright. One cannot have a copyright in one's image. But she may have other rights, rights relating to her privacy or publicity. Photographers, videographers, and others often carry "model" releases in their back pockets which they hand out and get signed on the street when doing a shoot in public. Although many think this model release relates to copyright, it relates to another area of law.

Those who create and own IP must be aware of rights that do not fall within the traditional definition of IP but which are nonetheless related and often important vis-à-vis digital property. Some of these rights are outlined below.

As is the case with all legal issues in this book, the law varies from jurisdiction to jurisdiction and country to country, and what is set out in this book are generalizations to warn you about certain issues. Further research and proper legal advice should be obtained where necessary.

Privacy and Publicity Rights

Privacy and publicity rights, while related, serve different purposes and possess distinct characteristics. The former protects individuals' privacy, whether physical or with respect to the details of their private lives. Publicity rights, however, are recognized to maximize the extent to which individuals may profit from their reputations and the recognition of their names and likenesses by preventing others from doing so.

Privacy

The best fame is a writer's fame: it's enough to get a table at a good restaurant, but not enough that you get interrupted when you eat.

— Fran Lebowitz

Privacy rights protect anonymity, control unwanted disclosures of private facts, and prevent embarrassment or harassment in domestic situations or for political purposes. These rights are balanced against societal rights such as freedom of expression. Whether privacy rights are recognized may depend on the extent to which the person alleging his infringement had reasonable expectations of privacy. Privacy rights can involve the misappropriation of someone's name or likeness, in which case they are invoked to seek compensation for the hurt feelings or embarrassment such misappropriation may cause. Since only living persons can suffer hurt feelings or embarrassment, no such rights survive death. In the case of deceased individuals, therefore, such as Elvis Presley, privacy rights are not applicable.

At least in the United States, four related tort[1] actions are involved in a privacy claim: appropriation of name or likeness, (physical) intrusion, public disclosure of private facts, and publicity which places the plaintiff in a false light in the public's perception. The truth or falsity of statements or facts involved is immaterial in cases involving breaches of privacy. Different criteria for a privacy claim would apply in different countries.

Publicity

> *Well, not exactly a big star. . . . But I once had a sandwich named after me at the Stage Delicatessen.*
>
> — Neil Simon, *The Gingerbread Lady*

Publicity rights, where recognized, are designed to compensate people for the commercial exploitation of their names or likenesses and to prevent unauthorized uses of a person's "persona" in relation to advertising and other forms of promotion. Persona may consist of a person's name (including identifying first names standing alone), pictures, likenesses (including drawings, caricatures, or cartoons), voices, or signatures. The right can be exercised by individuals or groups of individuals, the obscure as well as the famous.

Publicity rights are closely related to privacy rights and are recognized in various jurisdictions, including some U.S. states and Canadian provinces, as a form of property. However, instead of focusing on hurt feelings or embarrassment, they are designed to compensate people for the commercial exploitation of their names, likenesses, or images by enabling them to prevent their unauthorized use by others. In the case of living persons, therefore, written releases should be obtained from persons whose images are used. Otherwise, the "user" runs the risk of committing the tort of misappropriation of personality, for which damages can be sought and awarded.

In some jurisdictions, most notably various U.S. states, and in opposition to privacy rights, publicity rights can survive death and be enforced by the estates of deceased persons.

Defamation, Libel, and Slander

I love being a writer. What I can't stand is the paperwork.
— Peter de Vries

The law of defamation is designed to protect a person's reputation. According to *Black's Law Dictionary*, it applies when one is held up to "ridicule, scorn or contempt in a respectable and considerable part of the community" and includes both libel (written defamation) and slander (oral defamation).[2]

Even works of fiction, in certain circumstances, could be defamatory. While "publication" may be required before a defamation suit can proceed, all that it may entail is the communication of the defamatory statement to one person other than the plaintiff (i.e., the person allegedly being defamed). A defamatory comment or statement could be published in written form (libel), in oral form (slander), and perhaps even electronically published (that is, by transmission over the Internet). Note that the word *published* is being used here in the broad sense of "making generally known," rather than simply "producing a publication."

Regardless of the jurisdiction, the law of defamation can be a potent weapon in the protection of a person's reputation against untrue statements and something a creator or publisher should be aware of. Probably the most important question in any defamation claim is the notoriety of the plaintiff. The more public the figure, the more difficult it will be for him to succeed. Holders of elected office and famous celebrities are clearly public figures, but so too can private persons involved in a notorious event or even an accident become public figures.

Repetition of, and even reportings on, defamatory statements can attract independent liability, obviously something a new media entrepreneur needs to be concerned about. For instance, one must be concerned about "republishing" an article or parts of it in a Web site.

Pornography and Obscenity

Any work that contains sexually explicit materials, especially if visual and seemingly involving minors, can expose its author and/or publisher to obscenity charges. Whether material is considered obscene or pornographic varies from place to place and over time as the applicable legislation, penal or otherwise, and related community standards used to judge such questions evolve. As a result, it is difficult to provide a single definition of pornographic or obscene materials. If you are concerned that your works may contain any pornographic or obscene portions, contact a lawyer to help you determine how these phrases are interpreted in the applicable jurisdiction(s).

Union Fees

In addition to rights in copyright statutes, you need to be aware of reuse rights for performances, whether union or nonunion, and for any reuse fees or other payments required by contracts, collective agreements, or union rules. For example, if there is a film clip on your Web site and you have cleared the copyright in the film clip, you may also have to pay reuse fees to the performers' and musicians' unions (the Screen Actors Guild in the United States or the Alliance of Canadian Television and Radio Artists in Canada, and in both countries the American Federation of Musicians).

Trademarks

> *Just because Marilyn Monroe is dead doesn't mean she has to stop making movies.*
> — Salem Alaton, *Globe and Mail*[3]

The use of trademarks in association with digital property should be handled with the same diligence as the use of trademarks in association with traditional media. Marks should be used in association with the goods and/or services for which they are recognized and with a mention of the trademark's owner. For example, the name WordPerfect should only be used on that particular software, and Corel should be mentioned as the trademark owner where the WordPerfect mark is used.

If you own a trademark that is used by someone else, it's probably best to license in writing all uses of the trademark to ensure you maintain control over it. And as with your digital property, it's a good idea to periodically search the Net to see if anyone is using your trademark(s) without your permission, and to remedy any unauthorized uses by requesting that the trademark be removed from the Web site or by entering into a license agreement with the user.

Further, you should be careful if you use the trademarks of others without their permission. For instance, a common use of a trademark on a Web site is the inclusion of the mark with a link to that trademark owner's Web site. Whether including that trademark on your Web site would constitute use of a trademark may vary in different legal jurisdictions. If you're using someone else's trademark, don't be surprised if they ask you to sign a license agreement permitting you to include their mark on your site (which you might consider doing prior to being asked to do so, and rather than taking the risk of being sued for trademark infringement).

Idea Submission Releases

> *People also send him [John Grisham] ideas, and partly to guard against copyright infringement, he has a team of lawyers on retainer.*
>
> — Mel Gussow, *New York Times*[4]

What exactly is a submission release form? It is an agreement, usually signed by a creator submitting material, or "pitching" a concept or idea, to "release" the receiving party. The receiving party is usually a studio or production company, a director, developer, publisher, or actor who has asked the creator to sign this often one-sided agreement to release the receiving party from any obligation to the creator with respect to that particular submission or material. That being said, however, a release is not intended to protect a receiving party who intentionally steals your work, although proving that actual theft occurred may be difficult.

Generally, in a release, the creator acknowledges the fact that other persons may submit, and do submit, similar or identical material or ideas. As such, the receiving party is not liable to compensate the creator if they independently (of that particular creator) create and/or develop similar or identical material. Another provision in a release may make it clear that no confidential or fiduciary (trust) relationship exists between the creator and the person to whom the submission is sent — that is, the receiving party is not bound to treat the information as confidential.

Sometimes, the creator can attempt to include certain provisions in the release to protect himself. For instance, the creator might request that the recipient not disclose his idea to anyone else except to advance the pitched project within the company. Another provision could be one stipulating that the creator retains the right to submit the same materials to other persons. It should always be remembered, however, that releases are provided for the benefit of the receiving party. Given the power imbalances inherent in such a process, it can often be difficult for the creator to include many provisions to benefit himself.

Advertising and Promotion on the Internet

Because of the international nature of the Net, new media entrepreneurs must be cautious of customs and interpretations of words, phrases, and images around the world. And you should be aware of advertising laws in other countries from which a Web site might be accessed, as you may be subject to those laws when advertising in other countries. Further, if you have any games or contests on your Web site, different laws in different jurisdictions may apply.

One basic rule of advertising on the Net (and in a global market) is to stick to the truth. If you make truthful statements, backed up by facts, and you avoid misleading consumers and disparaging your competitors, you will be on safer ground. Avoid making product comparisons and omitting important facts, and make sure any links on your Web site do not mislead the customer about your products or services. Some jurisdictions have specific rules for advertisements aimed at children and restrictions on certain products like tobacco and alcohol. Lastly, it may be prudent to include a disclaimer in your advertisement that clearly states to what jurisdictions the advertisement is aimed.

Contractual Agreements

> *An original idea. That can't be too hard. The library must be full of them.*
>
> — Stephen Fry, *The Liar*

As you can see, in order to legally protect your digital property, you might enter into various contractual relationships. As such, you need to know the basic principles of contract law. From a lawyer's point of view, a contract or agreement is a tool to clarify a relationship at its inception, and a document which can help you avoid future conflict and even litigation by setting out the terms and conditions of your arrangements in advance. It is a document that you may return to from time to time to verify your original agreement and your rights and obligations, as well as the other party's rights and obligations, in the particular circumstances. It is also a useful tool for identifying all of the costs of a project and who is responsible for paying them.

What Is a Valid Contract?

When negotiating, drafting, or reviewing a contract, keep in mind that a valid contract has three components:

1. An offer to do something or refrain from doing something (for example, to purchase a print book, license computer software, or commission someone to design a Web site)

2. Acceptance of the offer

3. Consideration (consideration is something which is of some value in the eyes of the law — money is one example of consideration; a promise to supply goods or perform services is another)

Some Common Clauses

Any terms and conditions to which the parties agree, provided they do not contravene any specific laws, may be included in the contract. Some general provisions found in IP-related contracts are discussed below.

A contract should state the legal names and addresses of the parties who are subject to it. The contract should state the purpose of the contract (e.g., to license text, photographs, or computer software) and the rights and obligations of each party (e.g., the author will write a book in a certain genre at an approximate page length by a specific date, and the publisher will publish the book at its own expense and distribute it in Australia in the English language). The contract should discuss and clarify ownership of copyright. For instance, the author might retain copyright but license it to the publisher for two or maybe five years. It would be a term in the contract as to whether the author or publisher would have the right to publish it in French or adapt it into a film. Compensation (also known as "consideration" in legal jargon) must be mentioned. For example, the author could be entitled to 10 percent royalties on the retail price of each book sold, subject to specific deductions.

Further, the contract may have a number of general or boilerplate provisions relating to such things as arbitration, applicable law, bankruptcy, etc., many of which are listed and discussed in chapter 5.

The agreement should be signed by all parties to it. If you are contracting with a corporation, the signature should be of an authorized corporate officer, whose name, title, and the name of the corporation should be stated. It is also advisable to place the corporate seal on the agreement.

Although oral contracts may be legally binding in certain circumstances and in certain jurisdictions, this is not universally true. In addition, oral contracts are hard to prove, as they are usually one person's word against another's. Written agreements are always advisable.

Before signing a contract, review the wording of your contract with great care to ensure that it means only what you intend it to mean, and think that it means. Consult any organizations and/or unions in your artistic discipline for further information and sample contracts and consult a lawyer as well.

Online Contracts

An online contract is one created by email, through a Web site, or via electronic data interchange. Online contracts are possible, for example, for purchasing IP, and although they possess some unique features, they are not all that different from contracts formed via fax, which many people now take for granted. If you're using an online contract, don't forget to make a printout for your files and/or to retain a digital copy so that you can refer to it later.

Regulatory Areas of Law

Much of the discussion in this chapter refers to areas of the law which your contractual agreements may address. You should also be aware that governments around the world are reviewing various regulatory matters with regard to the Internet, which may have a direct or indirect impact on content owners. For instance, telecommunications laws may determine who may provide access to the Internet and the pace of bandwidth expansion. Also, laws and regulations may affect online content and regulate pornography. Encryption regulation may be important, especially in the United States. U.S. law-enforcement agencies have opposed liberalizing the U.S. policy that restricts the export of software that enables high levels encryption. They are concerned about foreign criminals who may use sophisticated encryption to escape detection.

The Copyright Lawyer

> . . . *I want to impress upon honourable gentlemen who are not lawyers the fact that the question of copyright is of importance not only to lawyers, but to many people in this country.*
> — Honorable George G. Foster, Canadian Senate (1919)

As you can gather, IP law is not a straightforward area of the law. What rights you license, for how long, exclusively or nonexclusively, in what territory, and at what price are complex and interwoven elements and will, of course, determine to what extent, financially and otherwise, you benefit from your digital property.

Sometimes you may handle legal or quasi-legal situations on your own, and in other circumstances you may engage a lawyer to help you out.

Whenever you engage a lawyer, you need to consider at what stage in any particular process (e.g., contract negotiation, non-payment issue, dispute over ownership) you should consult your lawyer. Some people involve their lawyer from the very beginning so that she can conduct all the negotiations on their behalf. Others prefer to deal with these matters themselves and merely have the "deal" reviewed by a lawyer before signing the agreement. Although you may save money by bringing in your lawyer at the end of the process, you may have missed some good advice in the negotiating stage that the lawyer is unable to correct by merely being responsible for reviewing or drafting an agreement. On the other hand, if you want to keep your costs down or create a more friendly atmosphere by not engaging lawyers, it is advisable to keep your lawyer informed along the way and perhaps use her as a sounding board and someone to keep you on track. Emotionally speaking, it may be better to have someone else negotiate on your behalf, who does not necessarily have to be a lawyer, but is experienced in the process. In some situations, where the other party already has a lawyer, it may be a good idea for you to have one too. Remember, though, that generally you are not required to retain a lawyer, even if you are involved in litigation.

If you have a lawyer working with you on the drafting of an agreement and the other party does not, you should consider insisting that he at least have the final agreement reviewed by an independent lawyer. This is very important because one lawyer should never represent, or purport to represent, various parties to an agreement. The other party cannot adopt your lawyer's advice as advice to him as well. This would be a conflict as each party is aiming, within reasonable bounds, to obtain the very best for him- or herself. If the other party signs the agreement without some legal input, he could later claim that the deal was unfair or that you exerted undue influence over him prior to signing it, and he could possibly have it set aside by a court of law. This is possible if the unrepresented party is "weak" or has lesser "bargaining power" or is "unsophisticated" in terms of the contractual agreements in question.

Finding a Lawyer

Before you can contact your lawyer, however, you must have one, or at least know one whom you could contact. Ask friends, colleagues, or professional associations in your field for recommendations. Also, contact your local bar association or law society to refer you to a lawyer experienced and competent to handle your legal issues. Some professional associations provide summary legal advice or names of lawyers who provide discounts to the association's members. You do not have to engage the first lawyer with whom you speak. You can call or meet with more than one lawyer. However, if you do "interview" lawyers in person, let them know in advance and ask whether the meeting is subject to a fee. In general, lawyers earn their income by charging by the hour, and although they may provide a free initial consultation in certain circumstances, they are generally not obligated to do so. Further, sole practitioners and law firms may provide different types of specialized and general legal services as well as different "atmospheres" and you may be more comfortable in dealing with a sole practitioner or a larger law firm depending on your preferences.

Copyright and IP are specialized and complex areas, and even if you have a lawyer who handles your real estate dealings, or wills, for example, she may not be the best lawyer for your IP needs. In fact, your "general" lawyer may be the first person to suggest an IP lawyer for your special needs. Neither should you assume that, just because a lawyer has expertise in one area of IP, she is automatically an expert in every area of IP. Some copyright lawyers know little about patents, and a trademark lawyer may not be the best person to draft an agreement for the licensing of Web site content.

Your Initial Meeting

When you meet with your lawyer, bring along everything even remotely related to the legal issues at hand. Even if you don't consider certain documents important, your lawyer may, and it would be better to provide her with everything at the beginning. Your lawyer will ask you to describe the fact situation that initiated the meeting and will question you about all of the circumstances in order to determine the relevant legal issues and possible recourse. If you've kept a diary or notes of the events (which is always advisable), provide it to your lawyer.

Fees

Generally, lawyers charge by the hour, or charge a set fee per type of work. In some countries, including the United States, they may claim a certain percentage of the "deal," such as a percentage of the contract price negotiated or damages awarded in litigation. Always ask for an estimate of time prior to engaging a lawyer on an hourly basis, or for the set fee or percentage in the other types of arrangements. An hourly rate of $350 may sound high, but keep in mind that if it takes the lawyer one hour to do the same work that a lawyer charging $200 an hour takes two hours to do, you are paying less with the higher charging lawyer. Also, keep in mind that some lawyers may allow for special fee arrangements for clients who are starting out and who have long-term potential.

Final Word

It's important to be aware of the various legal issues relating to your digital property and your rights and obligations. Thinking about them in advance can encourage you to take proper precautions to help avoid problems later on.

End Notes

1. A tort is a private or civil wrong or injury, other than a breach of contract, for redress of which a court can order an award of monetary damages.

2. With respect to a corporation, trade or corporate libel may be applicable as well. This involves statements which are false and which injure the business reputation of a corporation or its products (product disparagement). Knowledge of the falsity must be established, together with an intent to cause harm.

3. Salem Alaton, "Digital Imaging Transforms the Movies," *Globe and Mail*, 1 October 1996, p C2.

4. Mel Gussow, "Grisham's Escape into Legal Thrillers," *New York Times*, 31 March 1997, p. C11.

PART 5
The Future

CHAPTER 10
Who Rules Cyberspace?

I never could make out what those damned dots meant.

— Lord Randolph Churchill (on decimal points)

Where is a work "used" by someone on the Internet? Would it be used in the United States if it is uploaded or posted to a Web site in that country? Or would it be considered used in England if it is downloaded or saved onto a computer hard drive in England? And what if it is printed in New Zealand? The international protection of IP is based on the principle of "national treatment." This means that legal protection is in the country where the work is used. This seems simple enough if a book is photocopied or music performed at a concert; however, the same cannot be said of works on the Internet. It is not always clear where a work is actually used. As such, the distribution of digital property on the Internet raises interesting jurisdictional issues in terms of where that property is actually used and which country's laws should apply to that use.

Related problems of jurisdiction arise with respect to areas of the law other than copyright. For example, pornographic materials are judged according to community standards. What if your organization has a Web site with potentially pornographic materials? In the city of Birmingham, Alabama, community standards may find those materials pornographic while the same materials may not be considered pornographic in London, England.

The courts in various countries around the world are only beginning to deal with jurisdictional issues in relation to the Net. For example, in a court decision on July 16, 1996 , the defendant, the operator of a Web site located in Italy, was ordered by a U.S. court to either shut down its site or to prohibit U.S. users from accessing the site.[1] Each individual case must be decided on its own according to its particular circumstances. However, there are some interesting global initiatives to help protect the works of new media entrepreneurs and provide those creators with incentives to develop and exploit their digital property around the world.

New International Treaties

These initiatives include two new copyright treaties that set out international standards for the legal protection of digital property. These two new treaties, adopted in Geneva on December 20, 1996, after a three-week Diplomatic Conference on Certain Copyright and Neighboring Rights Questions, are exciting historical developments. Under the auspices of the World Intellectual Property Organization (WIPO), negotiators (governments and NGOs, or nongovernmental organizations) from some 160 countries reached agreement on the new treaties, called the WIPO Copyright Treaty and the WIPO Performances and Phonograms Treaty. They deal with copyright needs in the digital era and changing international copyright norms in light of new technologies. Copies of these two treaties are included in the appendices.

At the same conference, a third draft treaty prepared for purposes of the conference was not even discussed. This draft treaty would provide protection to electronic and nonelectronic databases not otherwise protected by copyright law because they lack sufficient skill, labor, and originality. However, it was agreed at the conference that further work would be done on a database treaty.

What the Treaties Say

In short, the two new treaties attempt to protect IP in a digital form and/or distributed by digital means. For instance, text, images, and music transmitted on the Internet are explicitly protected under the treaties.

Also included in the new treaties are obligations concerning technological measures. These provisions state that countries should have adequate legal protection and effective remedies against the circumvention of technological measures that are used to protect digital property. The treaties also contain obligations concerning rights management information. This means that member countries to the treaties must provide sanctions against the unauthorized removal or alteration of any electronic rights management information and against the unauthorized importation (for distribution or otherwise), broadcasting, or communication of works with the knowledge that electronic rights management information has been wrongly removed or altered. Rights management information is defined as "information which identifies the work, the author of the work, the owner of any right in the work, or information about the terms and conditions of use of the work, and any numbers or codes that represent such information, when any of these items of information is attached to a copy of a work or appears in connection with the communication of a work to the public."

The treaties do not, however, deal with the issue of who is liable for works used on the Internet without the permission of the content owner. In fact, this question of liability was not on the table at the Diplomatic Conference and remains a matter for regulation in each country, whether in statutes of law or through court decisions. In the meantime, new media entrepreneurs face difficulties determining against whom they should enforce their rights when their content is used without permission. Possible liable parties may be online services or Internet service providers, Web site owners, librarians (and others who aid individuals with respect to accessing content on the Net), and telephone companies.

Entry into Force of the Two Treaties

The two treaties are binding only on those states that actually join them. The treaties are open for signature until December 31, 1997, by any member state of WIPO and by the European Community, with either treaty entering into force three months after thirty instruments of ratification or accession by states have been deposited with the director general of WIPO. Countries may join one or both of the treaties and must have their laws in conformity with the treaties at the time they join. At the time of writing, the European Union Council of Ministers has formally adopted a decision authorizing the signing, on behalf of the European Union, of the two new treaties. As well, the treaty will be signed by all member states of the European Union before December 31, 1997. On July 28, 1997, President Clinton formally sent the two WIPO treaties to the Senate, accompanied by the associated implementing legislation.

From a practical perspective, the treaties do not directly provide new rights to creators and owners of content. What they do is set a minimum international standard; countries who want to be part of this international scheme of minimum protection for content creators and owners must amend their own laws to provide at least the rights set out in the treaties. For countries who conform with these minimum standards of protection, and who join the treaties, their citizens will have that same minimum protection in other countries who join the treaties. In light of the global nature of digital property, it is important that new media entrepreneurs have some level of consistency in the protection of their rights and works around the world. This is the underlying purpose of the treaties.

A Cyberspace Jurisdiction

Notwithstanding stronger international copyright laws (and the anticipated resulting stronger domestic copyright laws) to protect owners of digital property, an outstanding problem is the enforcement of rights. In other words, new media entrepreneurs require efficient legal recourse to enforce their rights when their digital property is used without their permission.

Since the issues raised by the Internet are so unique and are changing so rapidly, some commentators have suggested that existing laws and structures need to be reexamined to meet the demands of new technologies. Some propose a replacement of the "old" copyright system with a unique and independent legal regime all its own: a "cyberspace jurisdiction," or law of the Internet. Of particular interest for purposes of this book are the copyright aspects of a cyberspace jurisdiction, which is the focus of this section.

Let's first look at why the current system of protection of IP may be insufficient to deal with cyberspace issues.

➡ Electronic communication and dissemination is voluminous and may go beyond the capability of the laws or governments to control.

➡ The global nature of the Internet results in activities in one country or jurisdiction having instantaneous and simultaneous results, sometimes unintentionally, in other places in the world.

➡ Cyberspace lacks borders or jurisdictions, and it is difficult, if not impossible, to determine where an unauthorized use of digital property takes place.

➡ Where there is more than one infringing activity, each one may take place in a different jurisdiction. For example, a reproduction may occur where a work is scanned for publication on a Web site (for instance, in London, England), but when it is transmitted to another jurisdiction and printed there (let's say, Seattle, Washington), further unauthorized use of digital property may have occurred.

➡ The alleged infringer may not easily be identified as being from a certain jurisdiction, since email and Web site addresses don't necessarily reflect the geographical location of the owner. In fact, some people go so far as to say that email, Web pages, and chat lines do not exist anywhere, but rather that they exist "everywhere, nowhere in particular, and only on the Net."[2]

➡ The roles of the actual infringers are not clearcut, and their activities are sometimes difficult to classify. For example, instead of a single publisher transmitting works to various users, ". . . transmitters and receivers [can] switch roles interactively, and . . . be linked among themselves in fluid and variegated patterns. This flexibility can impact on both creation and dissemination at any and all points in increasingly global networks."[3]

➡ The current mechanisms, especially court systems, are very slow, especially in comparison to the relatively "fast" nature of the Internet. As well, judges are not always experts in the complicated technology of the Internet to which the complex copyright laws must be applied.

Online Mediation

While governments and courts of law are beginning to examine and deal with the problems caused by the current legal system in relation to "digital disputes," netizens (i.e., users of the Net) are experimenting with various online dispute resolution mechanisms. Several attempts are currently underway to test the efficacy of online mediation and alternative dispute resolution. Some are outlined below.

The Virtual Magistrate

The Virtual Magistrate (*http://vmag.law.vill.edu:8080/* or *http://vmag.vcilp.org/*) is a U.S. online arbitration mechanism jointly sponsored by the Cyberspace Law Institute (CLI) and the National Center for Automated Information Research (NCAIR). It has been based at Villanova Law School (in Philadelphia, Pennsylvania) since March 1996.

The Magistrate deals with copyright, other intellectual property law issues, and pornography-related complaints on the Internet. The arbitrators, who are not necessarily lawyers, are appointed by the American Arbitration Association and the Cyberspace Law Institute and receive training in arbitration techniques. In dealing with copyright disputes, their goal is to provide "rapid, initial resolution of computer network disputes."[4] The way the arbitration works is that if the parties agree to be bound by an arbitrator's decision, it would be legally binding in most other jurisdictions pursuant to the New York Convention, an international convention to which over one hundred countries belong and which recognizes arbitration contracts.

The first decision issued by the Virtual Magistrate, *Tierney and Email America*, VM Docket No. 96-0001 (08 May 1996), resulted in a recommendation that an offensive email message, which could be construed as promoting "spamming" or junk email, be removed from AOL.

So far, Internet service providers seem uninterested in online mediation, perhaps because they see it as an unwanted form of regulation or at least as a possible limitation on their actions in the future. As well, non-English-speaking arbitrators from other countries must be recruited if the Virtual Magistrate project is to have any international credibility.

The Cybertribunal

The francophone Cybertribunal (*http://www.cybertribunal.org/*), sponsored by the University of Montreal Law Faculty's Centre de recherche en droit public (CRDP), is a non-American, bilingual equivalent of the Virtual Magistrate. It offers arbitration and mediation services in French or English. Prerequisites for its use are the consent of both parties, questions of public order ("d'ordre public"), and an issue confined to the Internet. Intellectual property, including copyright, is one of the Cybertribunal's specialties. Issues dealt with involve the reproduction of works in cyberspace, the use of copyright works, enforcing copyright, authors' moral rights, and the use of databases.

The Online Ombuds Office

The Online Ombuds Office (*http://www.ombuds.org/*) is also funded by the National Center for Automated Information Research. It is particularly interested in helping settle disputes involving copyright and domain name trademark issues (among others). It arose less as a result of Internet-based litigation than as a response to the increasing population and number of conflicts occurring in cyberspace. The ombudspersons are assisted by technical advisors.

The Future of Online Dispute Mechanisms

Despite the good intentions behind online facilities that have recently emerged to solve digital property issues, there are potential problems with this method of resolution. One is the lack of physical contact between the mediating parties, which means that no one can send or receive visual clues or body language signals. These subtle forms of communication can sometimes enhance the mediation process. Another barrier is resistance by cyberspace citizens, who are not overly open to regulation of any kind on the Internet.

Nevertheless, there are many possible advantages to online mediation. It can be speedier and more convenient than arranging to meet in person, and the lack of physical contact — notwithstanding the absence of visual signals — can lessen the emotional element (in this respect, it is similar to mediation over the telephone). Cost benefits could also be substantial. Another advantage is the ability to facilitate discussions and negotiations between parties who could be in different physical locations (cities, states, or even countries) and different legal jurisdictions — a not uncommon situation in Internet disputes. Lastly, the written nature of the online mediation process, when conducted entirely via email, allows each party to formulate a clear position before responding.

To assist in online mediation, there could be a Web site with legal resources, an online archive of case precedents and relevant legal information, a reference librarian to assist the parties in researching legal issues relating to their dispute, and online discussions between the affected parties and their representatives. Communication via email could be enhanced by Internet telephone (or I-phone) conversations, as well as by video teleconferencing. The various discussions could lead to a resolution document drafted by the mediator, and emailed to the parties involved or their counsel for evaluation and comments.

Final Word

The new international copyright treaties will encourage countries to provide greater protection of digital property and, in so doing, motivate new media entrepreneurs to create and distribute digital property. However, the issue of enforcing rights in one's digital property remains. The intriguing concept of a cyberspace jurisdiction may help in this regard, although there are many practical, legal, and technological problems with it. Plus, if governments accept the need for a separate cyberspace regime or for self-regulating international organizations with powers to confront legal issues peculiar to the Internet, then cyberspace citizens will have to accept the idea of external controls being placed on their lawless wild west. Nevertheless, interesting experiments with online mediation and arbitration are emerging. For now, the question of who rules cyberspace remains open for discussion.

End Notes

1. *Playboy Enterprises, Inc.* v. *Chuckleberry Publishing, Inc.*, CANY, 687 F2d 563 (1982).

2. David R. Johnson, and David G. Post, "Law and Borders: The Rise of Law in Cyberspace," *http://www.cli.org/X0025_LBFIN.html.*

3. Paul Geller, "Conflicts of Laws in Cyberspace: Rethinking International Copyright in a Digitally Networked World," *Columbia-VLA Journal of Law and the Arts* 20, no. 4 (Summer 1996), p. 572.

4. Virtual Magistrate Project, press release, 21 May 1996, *http://vmag .law.vill.edu:8080.*

CHAPTER 11

The Future of Digital Property

I never think of the future. It comes soon enough.

— Albert Einstein

You can only predict things after they have happened.

— Eugène Ionesco, *Rhinoceros*

In many ways, the future is already here. Invisible property, IP, has a new and permanent place in our lives. It touches virtually every human endeavor from recreation and education to business, health, and communication. We are surrounded by digital assets — e-zines, databases, digitized images, computer software, Web sites, and audio and video clips. Some of these assets already exist in digital form, whereas others must be converted, or generated by digital means. By understanding the increased significance of digital property in our culture and society, we are closer to understanding its value. We are also more wary of protecting our IP.

When the Internet first became accessible to the public, many thought that there was no place for the protection of its content. It was thought that all content on the Internet should be available for free and that laws were unnecessary to protect it. However, every indication is that the pre-Internet laws that protect IP will survive and adapt with the evolving technology of the Internet and other new media. In December 1996, the WIPO Diplomatic Conference in Geneva ended the debate over whether IP should be protected in digital form. At the conference, some 160 countries agreed to minimum international standards for the protection of IP as digital property. As a result, it is likely that we will see changes in the copyright laws of many countries in the coming years. Notwithstanding this fact, copyright laws have proven themselves to be quite flexible and somewhat technology neutral in their application to new media and the Internet. Although some clarification of copyright laws may be necessary, the pre-Internet copyright principles continue to work whether we're talking about films and books or about new media such as Web sites or digitized photographs.

Determining the value of our digital property and establishing the terms and conditions under which someone can use it are among the most significant IP issues. Although certain standards exist in traditional media, there are as yet no industry standards for setting the price and conditions for the use of IP in digital media. The basic question, "How much is it worth?" is still perhaps the most difficult to answer. But the digital property business is taking off. Some content owners are demanding payment for digital uses of their works and are entering into license agreements on a case-by-case basis, establishing precedents that will help pave the path to future industry standards.

We are seeing business models emerge on the Internet, models that help new media entrepreneurs control the use of their digital property and ensure payment for it. These models, including advertising and various forms of electronic transaction, are in the experimental stages. However, they are already proving successful with respect to e-publishing of text and images and selling computer software and music on the Internet. Both businesses and consumers are gaining confidence in the new media. In part, this is due to new technologies like watermarking and encryption that allow for secure uses of digital property. But content owners generally do not want barriers to prevent the use of their work; rather, they want the public to have access to it. To that end, technology is providing secure payment systems to protect consumers on the Internet, as well as micropayment systems for the buying and selling of IP. The faster these systems are developed, the more likely that valuable content will proliferate on the Net and become available to the public.

Electronic commerce, as well as online delivery of IP (digital commerce), is taking its first steps. Those who are selling digital property have an advantage over vendors of physical products because the digital distributor generally sells his product for a modest amount of money — an amount that does not try the confidence of consumers in the security of an online transaction. Consumers are simply more confident with online purchases of less expensive property on the Internet.

Further, new and existing copyright collectives and e-rights agencies are beginning to collect royalties for the use of texts, visuals, and music on the Internet. It is likely that the role of these collectives will quickly expand, especially if they can offer both content owners and consumers a transparent payment system, which would be extremely helpful in managing IP in electronic formats.

What derives from all of this activity is an abundance of opportunities for new media entrepreneurs. A "digital property culture" has begun to develop. People are beginning to understand that digital property, as well as traditional forms of IP, have a unique value in our society. Owners of digital property are making greater efforts to control unauthorized use of their IP and continuously exploring ways to be compensated when others use it. Individuals and businesses are learning how to audit their resources and more diligently manage their invisible property.

So, just how valuable will this real estate of the future become? No one knows for certain. But what is certain is that demand drives up value. And, as digital media continues its exponential growth, the demand for content will be fueled. We can safely say, digital property is here to stay. On the Internet, content is everything. Creators and owners have the incentive to create and disseminate content, and will find the means to financially benefit from it. And if consumers continue to demand more and more, digital property may thus become the strongest currency of the twenty-first century.

A P P E N D I X A

WIPO Copyright Treaty

adopted by the Diplomatic Conference on December 20, 1996

Contents

Preamble

The Contracting Parties,

Desiring to develop and maintain the protection of the rights of authors in their literary and artistic works in a manner as effective and uniform as possible,

Recognizing the need to introduce new international rules and clarify the interpretation of certain existing rules in order to provide adequate solutions to the questions raised by new economic, social, cultural and technological developments,

Recognizing the profound impact of the development and convergence of information and communication technologies on the creation and use of literary and artistic works,

Emphasizing the outstanding significance of copyright protection as an incentive for literary and artistic creation,

Recognizing the need to maintain a balance between the rights of authors and the larger public interest, particularly education, research and access to information, as reflected in the Berne Convention,

Have agreed as follows:

Article 1
Relation to the Berne Convention

(1) This Treaty is a special agreement within the meaning of Article 20 of the Berne Convention for the Protection of Literary and Artistic Works, as regards Contracting Parties that are countries of the Union established by that Convention. This Treaty shall not have any connection with treaties other than the Berne Convention, nor shall it prejudice any rights and obligations under any other treaties.

(2) Nothing in this Treaty shall derogate from existing obligations that Contracting Parties have to each other under the Berne Convention for the Protection of Literary and Artistic Works.

(3) Hereinafter, "Berne Convention" shall refer to the Paris Act of July 24, 1971 of the Berne Convention for the Protection of Literary and Artistic Works.

(4) Contracting Parties shall comply with Articles 1 to 21 and the Appendix of the Berne Convention.

Article 2
Scope of Copyright Protection

Copyright protection extends to expressions and not to ideas, procedures, methods of operation or mathematical concepts as such.

Article 3
Application of Articles 2 to 6 of the Berne Convention

Contracting Parties shall apply *mutatis mutandis* the provisions of Articles 2 to 6 of the Berne Convention in respect of the protection provided for in this Treaty.

Article 4
Computer Programs

Computer programs are protected as literary works within the meaning of Article 2 of the Berne Convention. Such protection applies to computer programs, whatever may be the mode or form of their expression.

Article 5
Compilations of Data (Databases)

Compilations of data or other material, in any form, which by reason of the selection or arrangement of their contents constitute intellectual creations, are protected as such. This protection does not extend to the data or the material itself and is without prejudice to any copyright subsisting in the data or material contained in the compilation.

Article 6
Right of Distribution

(1) Authors of literary and artistic works shall enjoy the exclusive right of authorizing the making available to the public of the original and copies of their works through sale or other transfer of ownership.

(2) Nothing in this Treaty shall affect the freedom of Contracting Parties to determine the conditions, if any, under which the exhaustion of the right in paragraph (1) applies after the first sale or other transfer of ownership of the original or a copy of the work with the authorization of the author.

Article 7
Right of Rental

(1) Authors of

(i) computer programs;

(ii) cinematographic works; and

(iii) works embodied in phonograms, as determined in the national law of Contracting Parties,

shall enjoy the exclusive right of authorizing commercial rental to the public of the originals or copies of their works.

(2) Paragraph (1) shall not apply

(i) in the case of computer programs, where the program itself is not the essential object of the rental; and

(ii) in the case of cimematographic works, unless such commercial rental has led to widespread copying of such works materially impairing the exclusive right of reproduction.

(3) Notwithstanding the provisions of paragraph (1), a Contracting Party that, on April 15, 1994, had and continues to have in force a system of equitable remuneration of authors for the rental of copies of their works embodied in phonograms may maintain that system provided that the commercial rental of works embodied in phonograms is not giving rise to the material impairment of the exclusive right of reproduction of authors.

Article 8
Right of Communication to the Public

Without prejudice to the provisions of Articles 11(1)(ii), 11*bis*(1)(i) and (ii), 11*ter*(1)(ii), 14(1)(ii) and 14*bis*(1) of the Berne Convention, authors of literary and artistic works shall enjoy the exclusive right of authorizing any communication to the public of their works, by wire or wireless means, including the making available to the public of their works in such a way that members of the public may access these works from a place and at a time individually chosen by them.

Article 9
Duration of the Protection of Photographic Works

In respect of photographic works, the Contracting Parties shall not apply the provisions of Article 7(4) of the Berne Convention.

Article 10
Limitations and Exceptions

(1) Contracting Parties may, in their national legislation, provide for limitations of or exceptions to the rights granted to authors of literary and artistic works under this Treaty in certain special cases that do not conflict with a normal exploitation of the work and do not unreasonably prejudice the legitimate interests of the author.

(2) Contracting Parties may, in their national legislation, provide for limitations of or exceptions to the rights granted to authors of literary and artistic works under this Treaty in certain special cases that do not conflict with a normal exploitation of the work and do not unreasonably prejudice the legitimate interests of the author.

Article 11
Obligations concerning Technological Measures

Contracting Parties shall provide adequate legal protection and effective legal remedies against the circumvention of effective technological measures that are used by authors in connection with the exercise of their rights under this Treaty or the Berne Convention and that restrict acts, in respect of their works, which are not authorized by the authors concerned or permitted by law.

Article 12
Obligations concerning Rights Management Information

(1) Contracting Parties shall provide adequate and effective legal remedies against any person knowingly performing any of the following acts knowing, or with respect to civil remedies having reasonable grounds to know, that it will induce, enable, facilitate or conceal an infringement of any right covered by this Treaty or the Berne Convention:

(i) to remove or alter any electronic rights management information without authority;

(ii) to distribute, import for distribution, broadcast or communicate to the public, without authority, works or copies of works knowing that electronic rights management information has been removed or altered without authority.

(2) As used in this Article, "rights management information" means information which identifies the work, the author of the work, the owner of any right in the work, or information about the terms and conditions of use of the work, and any numbers or codes that represent such information, when any of these items of information is attached to a copy of a work or appears in connection with the communication of a work to the public.

Article 13
Application in Time

Contracting Parties shall apply the provisions of Article 18 of the Berne Convention to all protection provided for in this Treaty.

Article 14
Provisions on Enforcement of Rights

(1) Contracting Parties undertake to adopt, in accordance with their legal systems, the measures necessary to ensure the application of this Treaty.

(2) Contracting Parties shall ensure that enforcement procedures are available under their law so as to permit effective action against any act of infringement of rights covered by this Treaty, including expeditious remedies to prevent infringements and remedies which constitute a deterrent to further infringements.

Article 15
Assembly

(1)(a) The Contracting Parties shall have an Assembly.

(b) Each Contracting Party shall be represented by one delegate who may be assisted by alternate delegates, advisors and experts.

(c) The expenses of each delegation shall be borne by the Contracting Party that has appointed the delegation. The Assembly may ask the World Intellectual Property Organization (hereinafter referred to as "WIPO") to grant financial assistance to facilitate the participation of delegations of Contracting Parties that are regarded as developing countries in conformity with the established practice of the General Assembly of the United Nations or that are countries in transition to a market economy.

(2)(a) The Assembly shall deal with matters concerning the maintenance and development of this Treaty and the application and operation of this Treaty.

(b) The Assembly shall perform the function allocated to it under Article 17(2) in respect of the admission of certain intergovernmental organizations to become party to this Treaty.

(c) The Assembly shall decide the convocation of any diplomatic conference for the revision of this Treaty and give the necessary instructions to the Director General of WIPO for the preparation of such diplomatic conference.

(3)(a) Each Contracting Party that is a State shall have one vote and shall vote only in its own name.

(b) Any Contracting Party that is an intergovernmental organization may participate in the vote, in place of its Member States, with a number of votes equal to the number of its Member States which are party to this Treaty. No such intergovernmental organization shall participate in the vote if any one of its Member States exercises its right to vote and *vice versa*.

(4) The Assembly shall meet in ordinary session once every two years upon convocation by the Director General of WIPO.

(5) The Assembly shall establish its own rules of procedure, including the convocation of extraordinary sessions, the requirements of a quorum and,

subject to the provisions of this Treaty, the required majority for various kinds of decisions.

Article 16
International Bureau

The International Bureau of WIPO shall perform the administrative tasks concerning the Treaty.

Article 17
Eligibility for Becoming Party to the Treaty

(1) Any Member State of WIPO may become party to this Treaty.

(2) The Assembly may decide to admit any intergovernmental organization to become party to this Treaty which declares that it is competent in respect of, and has its own legislation binding on all its Member States on, matters covered by this Treaty and that it has been duly authorized, in accordance with its internal procedures, to become party to this Treaty.

(3) The European Community, having made the declaration referred to in the preceding paragraph in the Diplomatic Conference that has adopted this Treaty, may become party to this Treaty.

Article 18
Rights and Obligations under the Treaty

Subject to any specific provisions to the contrary in this Treaty, each Contracting Party shall enjoy all of the rights and assume all of the obligations under this Treaty.

Article 19
Signature of the Treaty

This Treaty shall be open for signature until December 31, 1997, by any Member State of WIPO and by the European Community.

Article 20
Entry into Force of the Treaty

This Treaty shall enter into force three months after 30 instruments of ratification or accession by States have been deposited with the Director General of WIPO.

Article 21
Effective Date of Becoming Party to the Treaty

This Treaty shall bind

(i) the 30 States referred to in Article 20, from the date on which this Treaty has entered into force;

(ii) each other State from the expiration of three months from the date on which the State has deposited its instrument with the Director General of WIPO;

(iii) the European Community, from the expiration of three months after the deposit of its instrument of ratification or accession if such instrument has been deposited after the entry into force of this Treaty according to Article 20, or, three months after the entry into force of this Treaty if such instrument has been deposited before the entry into force of this Treaty;

(iv) any other intergovernmental organization that is admitted to become party to this Treaty, from the expiration of three months after the deposit of its instrument of accession.

Article 22
No Reservation to the Treaty

No reservation to this Treaty shall be admitted.

Article 23
Denunciation of the Treaty

This Treaty may be denounced by any Contracting Party by notification addressed to the Director General of WIPO. Any denunciation shall take effect one year from the date on which the Director General of WIPO received the notification.

Article 24
Languages of the Treaty

(1) This Treaty is signed in a single original in English, Arabic, Chinese, French, Russian and Spanish languages, the versions in these languages being equally authentic.

(2) An official text in any language other than those referred to in paragraph (1) shall be established by the Director General of WIPO on the request of an interested party, after consultation with all the interested parties. For the purposes of this paragraph, "interested party" means any Member State of WIPO whose official language, or one of whose official languages, is involved and the European Community, and any other intergovernmental organization that may become party to this Treaty, if one of its official languages is involved.

Article 25
Depositary

The Director General of WIPO is the depositary of this Treaty.

A P P E N D I X B

WIPO Performances and Phonograms Treaty

adopted by the Diplomatic Conference on December 20, 1996

Contents

CHAPTER V: ADMINISTRATIVE AND FINAL CLAUSES

Preamble

The Contracting Parties,

Desiring to develop and maintain the protection of the rights of performers and producers of phonograms in a manner as effective and uniform as possible,

Recognizing the need to introduce new international rules in order to provide adequate solutions to the questions raised by economic, social, cultural and technological developments,

Recognizing the profound impact of the development and convergence of information and communication technologies on the production and use of performances and phonograms,

Recognizing the need to maintain a balance between the rights of performers and producers of phonograms and the larger public interest, particularly education, research and access to information,

Have agreed as follows:

CHAPTER I
GENERAL PROVISIONS
Article 1
Relation to Other Conventions

(1) Nothing in this Treaty shall derogate from existing obligations that Contracting Parties have to each other under the International Convention for the Protection of Performers, Producers of Phonograms and Broadcasting Organizations done in Rome, October 26, 1961 (hereinafter the "Rome Convention").

(2) Protection granted under this Treaty shall leave intact and shall in no way affect the protection of copyright in literary and artistic works. Consequently, no provision of this Treaty may be interpreted as prejudicing such protection.

(3) This Treaty shall not have any connection with, nor shall it prejudice any rights and obligations under, any other treaties.

Article 2
Definitions

For the purposes of this Treaty:

(a) "performers" are actors, singers, musicians, dancers, and other persons who act, sing, deliver, declaim, play in, interpret, or otherwise perform literary or artistic works or expressions of folklore;

(b) "phonogram" means the fixation of the sounds of a performance or of other sounds, or of a representation of sounds, other than in the form of a fixation incorporated in a cinematographic or other audiovisual work;

(c) "fixation" means the embodiment of sounds, or of the representations thereof, from which they can be perceived, reproduced or communicated through a device;

(d) "producer of a phonogram" means the person, or the legal entity, who or which takes the initiative and has the responsibility for the first fixation of the sounds of a performance or other sounds, or the representations of sounds;

(e) "publication" of a fixed performance or a phonogram means the offering of copies of the fixed performance or the phonogram to the public, with the consent of the rightholder, and provided that copies are offered to the public in reasonable quantity;

(f) "broadcasting" means the transmission by wireless means for public reception of sounds or of images and sounds or of the representations thereof; such transmission by satellite is also "broadcasting"; transmission of encrypted signals is "broadcasting" where the means for decrypting are provided to the public by the broadcasting organization or with its consent;

(g) "communication to the public" of a performance or a phonogram means the transmission to the public by any medium, otherwise than by broadcasting, of sounds of a performance or the sounds or the representations of sounds fixed in a phonogram. For the purposes of Article 15, "communication to the public" includes making the sounds or representations of sounds fixed in a phonogram audible to the public.

Article 3
Beneficiaries of Protection under this Treaty

(1) Contracting Parties shall accord the protection provided under this Treaty to the performers and producers of phonograms who are nationals of other Contracting Parties.

(2) The nationals of other Contracting Parties shall be understood to be those performers or producers of phonograms who would meet the criteria for eligibility for protection provided under the Rome Convention, were all the Contracting Parties to this Treaty Contracting States of that Convention. In respect of these criteria of eligibility, Contracting Parties shall apply the relevant definitions in Article 2 of this Treaty.

(3) Any Contracting Party availing itself of the possibilities provided in Article 5(3) of the Rome Convention or, for the purposes of Article 5 of the same Convention, Article 17 thereof shall make a notification as foreseen in those provisions to the Director General of the World Intellectual Property Organization (WIPO).

Article 4
National Treatment

(1) Each Contracting Party shall accord to nationals of other Contracting Parties, as defined in Article 3(2), the treatment it accords to its own nationals with regard to the exclusive rights specifically granted in this Treaty, and to the right to equitable remuneration provided for in Article 15 of this Treaty.

(2) The obligation provided for in paragraph (1) does not apply to the extent that another Contracting Party makes use of the reservations permitted by Article 15(3) of this Treaty.

CHAPTER II
RIGHTS OF PERFORMERS
Article 5
Moral Rights of Performers

(1) Independently of a performer's economic rights, and even after the transfer of those rights, the performer shall, as regards his live aural performances or performances fixed in phonograms, have the right to claim to be identified as the performer of his performances, except where omission is dictated by the manner of the use of the performance, and to object to any distortion, mutilation or other modification of his performances that would be prejudicial to his reputation.

(2) The rights granted to a performer in accordance with paragraph (1) shall, after his death, be maintained, at least until the expiry of the economic rights, and shall be exercisable by the persons or institutions authorized by the legislation of the Contracting Party where protection is claimed. However, those Contracting Parties whose legislation, at the moment of their ratification of or access to this Treaty, does not provide for protection after the death of the performer of all rights set out in the preceding paragraph may provide that some of these rights will, after his death, cease to be maintained.

(3) The means of redress for safeguarding the rights granted under this Article shall be governed by the legislation of the Contracting Party where protection is claimed.

Article 6
Economic Rights of Performers in their Unfixed Performances

Performers shall enjoy the exclusive right of authorizing, as regards their performances:

(i) the broadcasting and communication to the public of their unfixed performances except where the performance is already a broadcast performance; and

(ii) the fixation of their unfixed performances.

Article 7
Right of Reproduction

Performers shall enjoy the exclusive right of authorizing the direct or indirect reproduction of their performances fixed in phonograms, in any manner or form.

Article 8
Right of Distribution

(1) Performers shall enjoy the exclusive right of authorizing the making available to the public of the original and copies of their performances fixed in phonograms through sale or other transfer of ownership.

(2) Nothing in this Treaty shall affect the freedom of Contracting Parties to determine the conditions, if any, under which the exhaustion of the right in paragraph (1) applies after the first sale or other transfer or ownership of the original or a copy of the fixed performance with the authorization of the performer.

Article 9
Right of Rental

(1) Performers shall enjoy the exclusive right of authorizing the commercial rental to the public of the original and copies of their performances fixed in phonograms as determined in the national law of Contracting Parties, even after distribution of them by, or pursuant to, authorization by the performer.

(2) Notwithstanding the provisions of paragraph (1), a Contracting Party that, on April 15, 1994, had and continues to have in force a system of equitable remuneration of performers for the rental of copies of their performances fixed in phonograms, may maintain that system provided that the commercial rental of phonograms is not giving rise to the material impairment of the exclusive right of reproduction of performers.

Article 10
Right of Making Available of Fixed Performances

Performers shall enjoy the exclusive right of authorizing the making available to the public of their performances fixed in phonograms, by wire or wireless means, in such a way that members of the public may access them from a place and at a time individually chosen by them.

CHAPTER III
RIGHTS OF PRODUCERS OF PHONOGRAMS
Article 11
Right of Reproduction

Producers of phonograms shall enjoy the exclusive right of authorizing the direct or indirect reproduction of their phonograms, in any manner or form.

Article 12
Right of Distribution

(1) Producers of phonograms shall enjoy the exclusive right of authorizing the making available to the public of the original and copies of their phonograms through sale or other transfer of ownership.

(2) Nothing in this Treaty shall affect the freedom of Contracting Parties to determine the conditions, if any, under which the exhaustion of the right in paragraph (1) applies after the first sale or other transfer of ownership of the original or a copy of the phonogram with the authorization of the producer of the phonogram.

Article 13
Right of Rental

(1) Producers of phonograms shall enjoy the exclusive right of authorizing the commercial rental to the public of the original and copies of their phonograms, even after distribution of them by or pursuant to authorization by the producer.

(2) Notwithstanding the provisions of paragraph (1), a Contracting Party that, on April 15, 1994, had and continues to have in force a system of equitable remuneration of pro-ducers of phonograms for the rental of copies of their phonograms, may maintain that system provided that the commercial rental of phonograms is not giving rise to the material impairment of the exclusive rights of reproduction of producers of phonograms.

Article 14
Right of Making Available of Phonograms

Producers of phonograms shall enjoy the exclusive right of authorizing the making available to the public of their phonograms, by wire or wireless means, in such a way that members of the public may access them from a place and at a time individually chosen by them.

CHAPTER IV
COMMON PROVISIONS
Article 15
Right to Remuneration for Broadcasting and
Communication to the Public

(1) Performers and producers of phonograms shall enjoy the right to a single equitable remuneration for the direct or indirect use of phonograms published for commercial purposes for broadcasting or for any communication to the public.

(2) Contracting Parties may establish in their national legislation that the single equitable remuneration shall be claimed from the user by the performer or by the producer of a phonogram or by both. Contracting Parties may enact national legislation that, in the absence of an agreement between the performer and the producer of a phonogram, sets the terms according to which performers and producers of phonograms shall share the single equitable remuneration.

(3) Any Contracting Party may in a notification deposited with the Director General of WIPO, declare that it will apply the provisions of paragraph (1) only in respect of certain uses, or that it will limit their application in some other way, or that it will not apply these provisions at all.

(4) For the purposes of this Article, phonograms made available to the public by wire or wireless means in such a way that members of the public may access them from a place and at a time individually chosen by them shall be considered as if they had been published for commercial purposes.

Article 16
Limitations and Exceptions

(1) Contracting Parties may, in their national legislation, provide for the same kinds of limitations or exceptions with regard to the protection of performers and producers of phonograms as they provide for, in their national legislation, in connection with the protection of copyright in literary and artistic works.

(2) Contracting Parties shall confine any limitations of or exceptions to rights provided for in this Treaty to certain special cases which do not conflict with a normal exploitation of the perforFmance or phonogram and do not unreasonably prejudice the legitimate interests of the performer or of the producer of the phonogram.

Article 17
Term of Protection

(1) The term of protection to be granted to performers under this Treaty shall last, at least, until the end of a period of 50 years computed from the end of the year in which the performance was fixed in a phonogram.

(2) The term of protection to be granted to producers of phonograms under this Treaty shall last, at least, until the end of a period of 50 years computed from the end of the year in which the phonogram was published, or failing such publication within 50 years from fixation of the phonogram, 50 years from the end of the year in which the fixation was made.

Article 18
Obligations concerning Technological Measures

Contracting Parties shall provide adequate legal protection and effective legal remedies against the circumvention of effective technological measures that are used by performers or producers of phonograms in connection with the exercise of their rights under this Treaty and that restrict acts, in respect of their performances or phonograms, which are not authorized by the performers or the producers of phonograms concerned or permitted by law.

Article 19
Obligations concerning Rights Management Information

(1) Contracting Parties shall provide adequate and effective legal remedies against any person knowingly performing any of the following acts knowing, or with respect to civil remedies having reasonable grounds to know, that it will induce, enable, facilitate or conceal an infringement of any right covered by this Treaty:

(i) to remove or alter any electronic rights management information without authority;

(ii) to distribute, import for distribution, broadcast, communicate or make available to the public, without authority, performances, copies of fixed performances or phonograms knowing that electronic rights management information has been removed or altered without authority.

(2) As used in this Article, "rights management information" means information which identifies the performer, the performance of the performer, the producer of the phonogram, the phonogram, the owner of any right in the performance or phonogram, or information about the terms and conditions of use of the performance or phonogram, and any numbers or codes that represent such information, when any of these items of information is attached to a copy of a fixed performance or a phonogram or appears in connection with the communication or making available of a fixed performance or a phonogram to the public.

Article 20
Formalities

The enjoyment and exercise of the rights provided for in this Treaty shall not be subject to any formality.

Article 21
Reservations

Subject to the provisions of Article 15(3), no reservations to this Treaty shall be permitted.

Article 22
Application in Time

(1) Contracting Parties shall apply the provisions of Article 18 of the Berne Convention, *mutatis mutandis*, to the rights of performers and producers of phonograms provided for in this Treaty.

(2) Notwithstanding paragraph (1), a Contracting Party may limit the application of Article 5 of this Treaty to performances which occurred after the entry into force of this Treaty for that Party.

Article 23
Provisions on Enforcement of Rights

(1) Contracting Parties undertake to adopt, in accordance with their legal systems, the measures necessary to ensure the application of this Treaty.

(2) Contracting Parties shall ensure that enforcement procedures are available under their law so as to permit effective action against any act of infringement of rights covered by this Treaty, including expeditious remedies to prevent infringements and remedies which constitute a deterrent to further infringements.

CHAPTER V
ADMINISTRATIVE AND FINAL CLAUSES
Article 24
Assembly

(1)(a) The Contracting Parties shall have an Assembly.

(b) Each Contracting Party shall be represented by one delegate who may be assisted by alternate delegates, advisors and experts.

(c) The expenses of each delegation shall be borne by the Contracting Party that has appointed the delegation. The Assembly may ask WIPO to grant financial assistance to facilitate the participation of delegations of Contracting Parties that are regarded as developing countries in conformity with the established practice of the General Assembly of the United Nations or that are countries in transition to a market economy.

(2)(a) The Assembly shall deal with matters concerning the maintenance and development of this Treaty and the application and operation of this Treaty.

(b) The Assembly shall perform the function allocated to it under Article 26(2) in respect of the admission of certain intergovernmental organizations to become party to this Treaty.

(c) The Assembly shall decide the convocation of any diplomatic conference for the revision of this Treaty and give the necessary instructions to the Director General of WIPO for the preparation of such diplomatic conference.

(3)(a) Each Contracting Party that is a State shall have one vote and shall vote only in its own name.

(b) Any Contracting Party that is an intergovernmental organization may participate in the vote, in place of its Member States, with a number of votes equal to the number of its Member States which are party to this Treaty. No such intergovernmental organization shall participate in the vote if any one of its Member States exercises its right to vote and vice versa.

(4) The Assembly shall meet in ordinary session once every two years upon convocation by the Director General of WIPO.

(5) The Assembly shall establish its own rules of procedure, including the convocation of extraordinary sessions, the requirements of a quorum and, subject to the provisions of this Treaty, the required majority for various kinds of decisions.

Article 25
International Bureau

The International Bureau of WIPO shall perform the administrative tasks concerning the Treaty.

Article 26
Eligibility for Becoming Party to the Treaty

(1) Any Member State of WIPO may become party to this Treaty.

(2) The Assembly may decide to admit any intergovernmental organization to become party to this Treaty which declares that it is competent in respect of, and has its own legislation binding on all its Member States on, matters covered by this Treaty and that it has been duly authorized, in accordance with its internal procedures, to become party to this Treaty.

(3) The European Community, having made the declaration referred to in the preceding paragraph in the Diplomatic Conference that has adopted this Treaty, may become party to this Treaty.

Article 27
Rights and Obligations under the Treaty

Subject to any specific provisions to the contrary in this Treaty, each Contracting Party shall enjoy all of the rights and assume all of the obligations under this Treaty.

Article 28
Signature of the Treaty

This Treaty shall be open for signature until December 31, 1997, by any Member State of WIPO and by the European Community.

Article 29
Entry into Force of the Treaty

This Treaty shall enter into force three months after 30 instruments of ratification or accession by States have been deposited with the Director General of WIPO.

Article 30
Effective Date of Becoming Party to the Treaty

This Treaty shall bind

(i) the 30 States referred to in Article 29, from the date on which this Treaty has entered into force;

(ii) each other State from the expiration of three months from the date on which the State has deposited its instrument with the Director General of WIPO;

(iii) the European Community, from the expiration of three months after the deposit of its instrument of ratification or accession if such instrument has been deposited after the entry into force of this Treaty according to Article 29, or, three months after the entry into force of this Treaty if such instrument has been deposited before the entry into force of this Treaty;

(iv) any other intergovernmental organization that is admitted to become party to this Treaty, from the expiration of three months after the deposit of its instrument of accession.

Article 31
Denunciation of the Treaty

This Treaty may be denounced by any Contracting Party by notification addressed to the Director General of WIPO. Any denunciation shall take effect one year from the date on which the Director General of WIPO received the notification.

Article 32
Languages of the Treaty

(1) This Treaty is signed in a single original in English, Arabic, Chinese, French, Russian and Spanish languages, the versions in all of these languages being equally authentic.

(2) An official text in any language other than those referred to in paragraph (1) shall be established by the Director General of WIPO on the request of an interested party, after consultation with all the interested parties. For the purposes of this paragraph, "interested party" means any Member State of WIPO whose official language, or one of whose official languages, is involved and the European Community, and any other intergovernmental organization that may become party to this Treaty, if one of its official languages is involved.

Article 33
Depositary

The Director General of WIPO is the depositary of this Treaty.

Anti-Piracy Contact Information

Videos

Canadian Motion Picture Distributors Association
Toronto: 416-496-1843
Montreal: 514-692-0701
Langley, B.C.: 604-574-4126
Canada-wide hotline: 1-800-363-9166
All hotline calls are confidential, and they also monitor other piracy activities such as unauthorized performances.

U.S. Motion Picture Association (U.S. and worldwide)
Hotline: 1-800-NOCOPYS (622-6797)
Tel: 818-995-6600
Fax: 818-382-1785
Email: hotline@mpaa.org

Federation Against Copyright Theft (FACT - U.K. - Video only) 181-568-6646

Sound Recordings

Canadian Recording Industry
Association
1-800-668-8820
Email: criaky@interlog.com

Recording Industry Association
of America
Washington: 202-775-0101
Piracy hotline: 1-800-223-2328

British Phonographic Industry
Tel: 0171-287-4422
Fax: 0171-287-2252
Email: apu@bpi.co.uk (specifically
for anti-piracy)
24-hour anti-piracy answer phone:
0171-437-1493

Software Piracy

Canadian Alliance Against
Software Theft
Canada: 1-800-263-9700

Software Publishers Association
http://www.spa.org/
Argentina: 1-393-1111
Australia: 880-681-388
Brazil: 11-5505-5223
Canada and U.S.: 1-800-388-7478
Colombia: 1-281-2424
England: 1-71-5352-7999
Europe: 33-1-53-77-63-77 (Paris)
Hong Kong: 2525-6011
Japan: 0120-288-220
Korea: 080-744-4509
Malaysia: 800-3237
New Zealand: 0800-763-892
Philippines: 800-888-0101
Singapore: 800-337-6400
Thailand: 652-1827

Index